Showcasing the Third Reich

The Nuremberg Rallies

SHOWCASING THE THIRD REICH

THE
NUREMBERG
RALLIES

ANDREW RAWSON

First published 2012 by Spellmount,
an imprint of The History Press
The Mill, Brimscombe Port
Stroud, Gloucestershire, GL5 2QG
www.thehistorypress.co.uk

British Library Cataloguing in Publication Data.
A catalogue record for this book is available from the British Library.

ISBN 978 0 7524 6789 4

Typesetting and origination by The History Press
Printed in Great Britain

CONTENTS

INTRODUCTION

Every September between 1933 and 1938 the area around Dutzendteich Lakes, two miles south east of Nuremberg's old town, was the centre of attention in Nazi Germany. Tens of thousands of Party members descended on the city to attend the Party rally and participate in the range of meetings, parades and march pasts held across the city and the Rally Grounds. Over the years thousands of labourers worked on a range of projects, both improving existing structures and building new ones, until the Rally Grounds covered 11km². Thousands of others worked on the railways and the roads that brought the visitors to the Dutzendteich area or on the accommodation, the hotels and campsites.

The Nazis used the rallies to get their messages across to their supporters face-to-face in an age before television and the internet. They also used their meetings and parades to strengthen the sense of unity across the Party and across the Reich. They were a defining point in the Nazi calendar, one which the visitors went away from invigorated and ready to face new challenges set by their leaders.

How the rallies expanded from a single day event into a week-long extravaganza and how the grounds expanded from a couple of existing arenas into Albert Speer's vision for a huge range of structures is described in this book. Biographies of the architects are also included. The different organisations which took part and their leaders are discussed as well as the full programme of parades, march pasts and meetings.

It is hoped that the reader will gain an insight into the men who brought the rallies to Nuremberg and their motives. The Nuremberg Laws, the Nazis way of dividing society into Aryans and non-Aryans, are part of the story and can be considered as an early step on the road to the Holocaust. Finally, what can still be seen today in Nuremberg is described and a tour around the Rally Grounds and the city centre is suggested.

1

The Rise of the Nazis and their Rallies

What follows is a brief description of the rise of the Nazis between the first rally in 1923 and the final, cancelled rally in 1939. It outlines each rally, illustrating how it developed from a simple day-long fund raising event into a week-long programme of activities.

THE FIRST PARTY CONGRESS (MUNICH, 27 JANUARY 1923)

20,000 supporters attended the first Party Rally in Munich on 27 January 1923. The SA's first four standards were consecrated during an ad-hoc ceremony; such ceremonies became an important part of future rallies. The Rally was a financial success and the NSDAP leaders decided to hold a second convention in the autumn.

THE GERMAN DAY RALLY (NUREMBERG, 1–2 SEPTEMBER 1923)

A two-day event was held in Nuremberg to make it easier for northern members to attend and it was called German Day to increase the appeal to the public. The rally focused on remembering two German military triumphs; the Battle of Sedan in 1870 against the French during the Franco-Prussian War and the Battle of Tannenberg against the Russians in 1914 during the First World War.

The SA demonstrated their discipline and comradeship, aiming to attract new members from other right-wing groups, and the highlight was a parade past Hitler, Erich Ludendorff and Julius Streicher in the Hauptmarkt. Eight weeks later, the three tried to seize power in Munich but the uprising failed and Hitler was jailed for five years in April 1924.

Alfred Rosenberg stood in as leader of the NSDAP but he was neither a leader nor an administrator and the Party soon broke up. The National Socialist Freedom Party was formed in April 1924 and a month later nearly two million people voted for it, putting 32 delegates in the Reichstag. Members of the SA also continued to meet under the guise of sports clubs, singing clubs and rifle clubs.

The march through the centre of Nuremberg was one of the early rituals.

THE SECOND PARTY CONGRESS, THE REFOUNDING CONGRESS (WEIMAR, 3–4 JULY 1926)

Hitler was released from prison on 24 December 1924 after serving only eight months. The ban on the NSDAP was lifted on 16 February 1925 and Hitler began work on uniting the Party across Germany. He faced opposition from Gregor and Otto Strasser in Berlin but they were brought into line at the Bamberg Conference on 14 February 1926.

Although the Party did not have enough funds to hold a Party Rally in 1925, members worked hard to raise money for one the following summer. Hitler was banned from speaking in Bavaria so it was moved to Weimar, Thuringia. The choice was a pragmatic one. Bavaria was out of bounds and the Bavarians in the Party did not want to hold the rally in Berlin. Weimar was the city where the National Congress had met in 1919 to establish a new post-war republic; the German Reich is often referred to as the Weimar Republic.

A new ceremony became a centrepiece of the rally when the battle-scarred flag carried during the 1923 Munich Putsch was paraded as a sacred relic. As the faithful looked on, Hitler held the Blood Flag, as it was called, and seized each new unit flag in turn, in a pseudo-religious consecration ceremony.

THE THIRD PARTY CONGRESS, THE DAY OF AWAKENING (NUREMBERG, 19–21 AUGUST 1927)

When Bavaria lifted its ban on Hitler speaking, the NSDAP returned to Nuremberg for their next annual congress. The city's favourable geographic situation and good rail links made it easier for supporters to get to the rally. It was a neutral city, which neither alienated the Bavarians nor the Prussians. Luitpold Grove (Luitpoidhain) was a practical meeting place and while Franconia had a well organised NSDAP under Julius Streicher, the Nuremberg police chief, Benno Martin, was sympathetic to the Nazi cause.

While the 1927 rally was a success, the NSDAP was spending all its money on campaigning. There was no rally in 1928 and the party instead focused on its leader conference in Munich.

THE FOURTH PARTY CONGRESS, THE DAY OF COMPOSURE (NUREMBERG, 2 AUGUST 1929)

By September 1929 the Party had increased its membership and subscriptions sufficiently to stage another rally. The NSDAP had recently allied itself with the German National People's Party (DNVP) to campaign against the Young Plan, a new financial plan designed to restructure Germany's war reparations. While the alliance did not last for long, the campaign increased the NSDAP's exposure due to favourable coverage in Alfred Hugenberg's newspapers.

The early rallies were disorganised affairs compared to the later ones.

Thousands of NSDAP members gathered in Nuremberg but the parades and marches drew the attention of the local Communist and Social Democrat supporters. There were clashes across the city, leaving the police struggling to keep control and street battles left two dead and many injured, including five policemen. The riots were covered extensively in newspapers, giving the Rally free publicity.

The Rally caused so much trouble that the city council banned future political conventions. They need not have bothered; the NSDAP was again out of money because campaigning had reached fever pitch. It had to be satisfied with holding leader conferences.

THE FIFTH PARTY CONGRESS, THE RALLY OF VICTORY (31 AUGUST–3 SEPTEMBER 1933, NUREMBERG)

Between August 1929 and August 1933 the NSDAP rose from strength to strength on the back of political unrest in Germany. It started with the Wall Street Crash in October 1929, when the value of the United States stock market fell rapidly, seriously undermining Germany's weak economy. As unemployment rose and businesses closed, support for Germany's democratic parties declined as voters looked to radical political parties for answers.

While support for the NSDAP rose during the Reichstag elections, Hitler's exposure increased because he stood in the Presidential elections. As Hitler flew around the country to meet the people, Party members campaigned hard and the SA's brown shirts fought opponents on the streets. By the end of 1932, the NSDAP was in a strong position while the leaders of the democratic parties were finding it impossible to solve the country's problems.

Hitler was appointed Chancellor at the head of a new cabinet on 30 January 1933. Four weeks later the Reichstag was burned down, civil rights were suspended and draconian measures were implemented. In March the Enabling Act was voted in, allowing the Cabinet to deviate from the Constitution's system of government and pass new laws. It also allowed the Nazis to amend Reich, State and local government to their own advantage.

In Nuremberg, Mayor Hermann Luppe was forced to resign on 16 March and was then arrested. The takeover of the city council by the NSDAP followed, opening the way for the organisation of a Party Rally. After years of resistance from the city council concerning

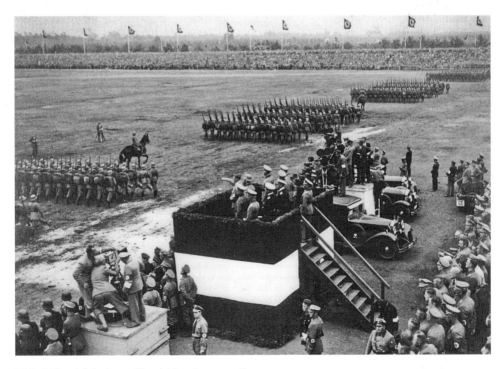

Makeshift stands had to suffice during the 1933 rally.

the disruption caused by the rally, the new Nazi council gave it their full backing and work on the rally grounds began in earnest.

The 1933 rally was the first to have an official title, the 'Rally of Victory', in honour of the victory of National Socialism over the Weimar Republic; effectively the victory of a dictatorship over democracy. The organisers erected temporary wooden platforms on Luitpold Arena and Zeppelin Field while Luitpold Hall was given a theatrical makeover. Hitler wanted a permanent record of the rally and he invited the film director Leni Riefenstahl to film a documentary called the 'Victory of Faith' or *Sieg des Glaubens*.

THE SIXTH PARTY CONGRESS, THE RALLY OF THE WILL
(5–10 SEPTEMBER 1934)

As soon as the 1933 rally ended, work started on turning Dutzendteich Parks into a dedicated area for Party rallies. Work started on permanent grandstands for the Luitpold Arena and the Zeppelin Arena while the facilities in Luitpold Hall were improved.

However, these improvements were only temporary because Albert Speer became responsible for the Rally Grounds on 25 April 1934 and he had grand designs. While local architect Ludwig Ruff was commissioned to build a new Congress Hall in June, Speer was looking at the bigger picture. With the number of visitors expected to increase rapidly, new accommodation and infrastructure had to be considered.

Meanwhile, problems with the leadership of the SA had been simmering for a time and on 30 June 1934 Ernst Röhm and many other SA leaders were arrested and executed by its rival organisation, the SS. Other opponents and rivals to Hitler were also eliminated during the Night of the Long Knives. It meant that the SA's new leader, Viktor Lutze, would stand alongside Hitler and Reichsführer SS, Heinrich Himmler, during future rallies.

The 1934 rally had several names celebrating the Party's unity in the wake of the Night of the Long Knives; the 'Rally of Unity and Strength', the 'Rally of Power' or the 'Rally of the Will'.

With Ernst Röhm's image banned across Germany, Hitler again asked Leni Riefenstahl to make a new film, drawing on lessons learnt from the first. This time she was involved in the planning and the result was the famous, or rather infamous, 'Triumph of the Will'.

THE SEVENTH PARTY CONGRESS, RALLY OF FREEDOM
(10–16 SEPTEMBERS 1935)

Construction work on the Rally Grounds continued at a furious pace following the 1934 rally. Albert Speer also produced a new plan in December outlining how the different structures, both existing and planned, would be connected by a huge road. He also planned a massive arena called the Mars Field.

The temporary grandstands on the Luitpold Arena and the Zeppelin Field had been replaced by permanent ones while similar improvements had been made to the terracing.

An advertising poster for the 1934 rally.

Work had also started on the new Congress Hall, turning the area around the Dutzendteich Lake into a gigantic construction site. A new, huge open air stadium called the German Stadium was planned to be added later.

The 1935 rally was designated the Rally of Freedom and the title celebrated the reintroduction of conscription, which had been banned under the 1919 Treaty of Versailles. The Luftwaffe also made an appearance for the first time, having been unveiled in March.

Honouring the war dead and the Nazi martyrs was one of the main rituals.

The 1935 rally will always be associated with the declaration of the anti-Semitic Nuremberg Laws. These new laws divided German society into citizens of the State and subjects of the State. They also banned marriages and sexual relations between Aryans and Jews.

THE EIGHTH PARTY CONGRESS, THE RALLY OF HONOUR (NUREMBERG, 8–14 SEPTEMBER 1936)

While the finishing touches were made to to the Luitpold Arena and the Zeppelin Field, work continued at a feverish pace on the Congress Hall foundations over the winter of 1935/36. Large tracts of woodland were cut down and the marshes were drained around the Dutzendteich Lakes to make way for Speer's new structures, including the Great Road, the Mars Field and the Langwasser campsite.

The Nazis' commitment to Nuremberg was confirmed on 7 July 1936 when the city was designated the 'City of the Reich Party Conventions'. The rally was called the Rally of Honour, in recognition of the occupation of the demilitarised zone of the Rhineland the previous March. Visitors were reminded that German troops grouped under the Condor Legion had been deployed to Spain to help General Franco's Nationalist troops in their Civil War with Republicans.

The Nazis also announced their Four-Year Plan, a sweeping economic reorganisation to make Germany financially and agriculturally independent. Shortly after the rally, Hermann Göring was given control of all aspects of the German economy.

THE NINTH PARTY CONGRESS, THE RALLY OF WORK (NUREMBERG, 6–13 SEPTEMBER 1937)

The 1937 rally was dedicated to the reduction of unemployment across Germany. The Depression had doubled unemployment from 2.9 million in 1929 to 6 million in 1933; a staggering 30 per cent of the workforce. By the end of 1937 the Nazis had reduced it to one million. However, all was not what it seemed. Construction schemes accounted for 500,000 men, 200,000 had been conscripted into the Reich Labour Service and another 750,000 had been conscripted in the armed forces. 800,000 women had also been forced out of the labour market. The Nazis' promise to reduce unemployment was met through compulsory employment and conscription rather than through effective economic policies. The increase of military-related industries and the recovery of the world markets from the effects of the Wall Street Crash also worked in their favour.

Visitors would have noted that the final touches had been made to the Luitpold Arena and the Zeppelin Field, while the foundations for the Congress Hall were complete. Extensive clearance works on the Great Road were still ongoing while the excavation for the German Stadium had only just started. Excavation works on the west side of the Mars Field had also been underway for twelve months.

The headquarters of the Rally organisation committee.

A new award was announced on the second day of the Congress, the German National Prize for Art and Science. The Nobel Peace Prize had been awarded to anti-Nazi author Carl von Ossietsky in 1935 and the Nazis banned Germans from accepting future awards. The German National Prize replaced it; only nine were awarded between 1937 and 1939.

The 1937 rally followed the format of the previous year with one notable exception, the spectacle of Speer's Cathedral of Light over the Zeppelin Field; a night-time light show created using dozens of searchlights. Parts of the rally were filmed and they were incorporated with footage from the 1938 rally to make a short film called *Festliches Nürnberg* or 'Festive Nuremberg'.

THE TENTH PARTY CONGRESS, THE RALLY OF GREATER GERMANY (5–12 SEPTEMBER 1938)

The 1938 rally was named in honour of the Union, or Anschluss, with Austria, creating a Greater Germany. Hitler was Austrian and he had wanted to merge his homeland with Germany for some time. He tried to bully the Chancellor of Austria, Kurt Schuschnigg,

'The New Line' or Great Road, which was to link the Rally Grounds with the city.

into working with him but failed. German troops crossed the Austrian border on 12 March and crowds turned out to greet them as they drove to Vienna. 200,000 Austrians turned out to hear Hitler proclaim the Union in the city. Artur Seyss-Inquart was appointed Chancellor and Nazi-style law and order was immediately implemented across Austria. The Union was overwhelmingly ratified by Austrian voters on 10 April.

The Nazis moved the Imperial Regalia, relics which belonged to the Emperors and Kings of the Holy Roman Empire, to St Katherine's Church in the centre of Nuremberg. Most of the relics had been brought to the city in 1426 but Napoleon's troops moved them to Vienna's Hofburg Palace in 1796. The collection included the Imperial Crown, Cross, Sword and Orb; it also included the Holy Lance and relics of the True Cross. The Nazis planned to display them in the new Congress Hall but it was never finished; they were returned to Vienna after the war.

Hitler had also been planning to invade Sudetenland, Czechoslovakia, since the September 1937 rally. Once Germany and Austria had been joined, he wanted to include the Sudeten Germans in the Third Reich. On 30 May 1938 Hitler secretly told his generals to prepare to cross the Czech border on 1 October and announced his intentions during the September 1938 rally.

A new day was added to the 1938 rally, the Day of Beauty. For the first time young men and women performed athletic exercises on the Zeppelin Field.

THE ELEVENTH PARTY CONGRESS, THE RALLY OF PEACE (PLANNED FOR 2–11 SEPTEMBER 1939)

All across the Rally Grounds thousands of labourers resumed work at a furious pace following the 1938 Rally, particularly on the Congress Hall and the SS Barracks at the north end of the Rally Grounds and the German Stadium and the Mars Field to the south. The city zoo was also moved to make way for buildings west of the new Congress Hall; it was moved to its present site at Schmausenbuck, east of the city centre.

The organisers planned a bigger and better rally for 1939; however, Hitler had other plans for September 1939. While Nuremberg was preparing for the Rally of Peace, Hitler was preparing for war. He had explained his plans to the heads of the armed forces on 5 November 1937 and from then on all his plans were focused on war.

Following Hitler's announcement that he intended to invade the Sudetenland, British Prime Minister, Neville Chamberlain and French Premier, Edouard Daladier, agreed to hand over the area to Germany to prevent a European war. Chamberlain declared 'I believe it is peace for our time.'

On 1 October German troops occupied the mountainous Sudetenland region; some of them had paraded at Nuremberg only four weeks earlier. Nazi law and order was imposed across the area and on 4 December the invasion was ratified. However, Hitler had not finished and on 15 March German troops marched into Slovakia, heading for Prague.

As early as 3 April 1938 Hitler had ordered the Wehrmacht to prepare to invade Poland on 1 September 1939 and he opened discussions with the leader of the Soviet Union,

Advertising the Rally of Peace, the rally cancelled due to war.

Joseph Stalin, when Czechoslovakia was secure. Joachim von Ribbentrop and Vyacheslav Molotov signed a pact on 23 August and while they openly agreed not to attack each other, they also secretly agreed to divide Poland in two. All that was needed was an excuse to attack and staged incidents along the border, with the main one near Gleiwitz on 31 August 1939, provided one. The following morning German troops crossed the border. The 1939 Rally of Peace was planned to start a day later. Rather than heading to Nuremberg, German troops were heading for Warsaw.

2

DEVELOPING THE LAYOUT OF THE RALLY GROUNDS

THE DUTZENDTEICH AREA BEFORE 1933

The Dutzendteich area was an important recreational area for the people of Nuremberg before the Nazis turned it into a huge construction site. At the end of the nineteenth century a bar, a bathhouse and boardwalk were built alongside the lakes for the public to enjoy. The annual Bavarian Exhibition was traditionally held on the Maxfeld, northeast of the city, but the park was becoming too small for the event by the turn of the century. 1906 was going to be the centenary of Nuremberg joining Bavaria and the city wanted to increase the size of the fair to commemorate the occasion. The city and the state were joined by businesses and fine arts organisations and between them they contributed five million Marks towards new exhibition grounds. The money was spent on a new, larger area between Wodanstraße and Dutzendteich Lakes, south east of the city centre.

An extensive area was cleared and levelled for the grounds and a huge exhibition building was constructed for a host of agriculture, industrial, commercial and art displays. Between May and October 1906 two and a half million people visited the exhibition, making the centenary celebrations a success.

The exhibition grounds were converted into a recreational park and called Luitpold Grove, fulfilling Nuremberg City Council's long-term plan to have a new park. The Grove soon became a popular weekend destination in the summer months and a regular funfair was soon visiting. Nuremberg Zoo also opened on the north side of Dutzendteich Lake in 1912 and it became the largest zoo in southern Germany; around 800,000 visitors came to see the animals in the first twelve months.

The main exhibition building of steel and glass was left standing and while it was initially called Prince Regent Hall it was later named Luitpold Hall. Luitpold had been named Regent of Bavaria when his nephew, King Ludwig II, was declared mentally incompetent in 1886; Luitpold ruled until his death in 1912.

Luitpold Hall was a useful venue and over the next 16 years it was used for a wide variety of events. There was a Workers Gymnastics Festival in 1910 and the centennial celebration of the Battle of Leipzig in 1913. Following the First World War, the hall was used

The 1906 Bavarian Exhibition on Luitpold Grove.

for political meetings and the Socialists and Independent Socialists held a joint rally inside in 1922. The following year the Social Democrats (SPD) held a rally in the hall, declaring the party's loyalty to the Weimar Republic. However, after 1927 the NSDAP became associated with Luitpold Grove. They staged rallies there in 1927 and 1929 and would have held more if the city had not banned on them following violent clashes.

Mayor Hermann Luppe also pushed for a modern sporting venue and the chosen location was on the south side of the Dutzendteich Lakes. Once the marshland had been drained, work started on an open air arena surrounded by earth terraces for spectators. The Zeppelin Field was a relatively straightforward arena to build and it was completed in 1921.

Nuremberg's Director of the Parks Department, Alfred Hensel (1880–1969) submitted plans for the rest of the area in 1923. The aim was to keep as much of the woodland as possible around an athletics arena, an outdoor swimming pool and a large lawn. Hensel planned gardens and children's playgrounds as well as a cafe and restaurant.

The track and field arena was designed by Otto Ernst Schweizer, one of Germany's leading architects. It was a modern, functional design and had an octagonal sports arena surrounded by a large grandstand for 50,000 spectators; 2500 seated under the large canti-lever roof of the stadium.

When they were finished, Nuremberg had one of the world's largest modern outdoor facilities, measuring around 300 hectares. All but the swimming pool were free (except during sporting events), making it a popular recreation area and tourist attraction. However, Nuremberg wanted to showcase its leisure facilities.

Hensel had planned some of the facilities for the 1928 Amsterdam Olympic Games and he received an Olympic gold medal for his contribution. Nuremberg wanted to stage the Games in 1936 and Hensel helped to put forward the city's application in 1929. Berlin won and the XIth Olympiad Games would forever become associated with the Nazi regime. So would Nuremberg, but it would be for a different kind of event; the Reich Party Congress – and for postwar reckonings.

The Franken Stadium in the foreground and the Zeppelin Field in the background.

NAZI PLANS FOR THE DUTZENDTEICH AREA

The NSDAP press portrayed Hitler as an inspirational architect who was intimately involved in the design of the Rally Grounds. One source summed up his involvement: 'Only he can plan; only he can build and act so big and so easy. The Führer is interested in even the smallest little things. He seeks out the material, the stone, he meets all his decisions; he plans just about everything. So it's his work, which exudes his spirit.'

While that was the official line, Hitler had very little input into the design of the Rally Grounds, either with the layout or with individual structures. Albert Speer, Ludwig and Franz Ruff, and the Nuremberg City Building Department designed everything. The Führer only approved or amended their plans, often when the construction was well underway.

Ludwig Ruff was well advanced in his plans for the new Congress Hall when Albert Speer became involved in the Rally Grounds on 25 April 1934. Work on the Luitpold Arena and Zeppelin Field was well underway and Speer's first input was to try and get the city council to illuminate the Zeppelin Field. He failed this time but he would succeed later.

Speer produced his first plan in October 1934, not long after the successful September rally. No changes were made to the Luitpold Arena, while the new Congress Hall was

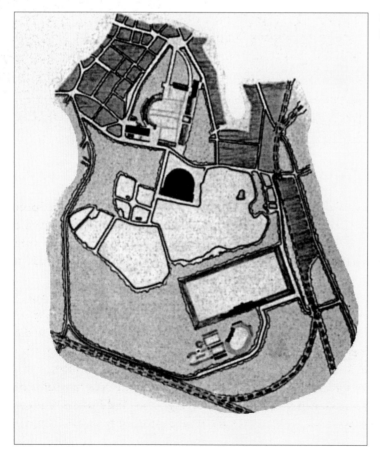

Speer's October 1934 plan.

Albert Speer explains
his plans to Hitler and
Rudolph Hess.

shown on the north side of Dutzendteich Lake, with the entrance facing south. Speer
also wanted to triple the size of the Zeppelin Field, with a new grandstand in the centre
of the south side. Speer's plan was a simple upgrade of what was already there; three
unconnected buildings scattered around a lake. There were no connecting roads and no
facilities for visitors.

In December 1934 Speer put forward a new plan for the Rally Grounds and it would
be the blueprint for construction until the war brought work to an end. Again, Luitpold
Arena remained the same but the Congress Hall had been turned through 90 degrees so the
delegates' entrance overlooked a new plaza. A collection of structures, including a Triumphal
Arch, a Cultural Hall and two obelisks stood on the north and west sides of the plaza.

While the extension to the Zeppelin Field had been dropped (possibly because of poor
ground conditions), Speer planned a replacement, the huge Mars Field to the south. A
wide paved highway, known as the Great Road, ran in a straight line from the Congress
Hall to the Mars Field.

Speer had also considered travel arrangements and accommodation for visitors for the first time. The railway station behind the Zeppelin Field had been upgraded and a road connected it to a huge campsite south of the Mars Field where five areas were sketched out for different Party organisations.

Speer's plan was based on the lessons from the previous rallies and it addressed many problems. It also involved levelling large areas of woodland and reshaping the lakes. However, little was done before the 1935 rally and a revised plan was put forward in November. The rally organisers were struggling to cope with the numbers of visitors and Speer increased the size of the campsites accordingly. He also added a second railway station between the Mars Field and the campsites.

Work continued at a fast pace until Germany invaded Poland in September 1939.

Although Luitpold Arena and Zeppelin Field had not been changed, the size of the Mars Field had been increased. Speer had also added the German Stadium, an open air stadium capable of seating 400,000 spectators. The massive structure was on the west side of the Great Road, looking towards the Zeppelin Field. The structure was a typical Hitler fantasy that Speer would attempt to turn into reality.

With all the structures in place, work on the Rally Grounds began in earnest and continued until the German Armed Forces invaded Poland in 1939. While hundreds of labourers were conscripted, the management teams believed work would resume following Poland's defeat and they continued to stockpile materials, ready for their return. They did not and the invasion of France in May 1940 followed by the planned invasion of England in the summer meant they never would. Speer's dream for a Rally Grounds to impress the world had evaporated.

Even so, Hitler's architect continued tweaking the layout, focusing on linking the Rally Grounds to the city centre, and he reissued them in February 1941. Although the changes looked minimal on paper they involved huge changes on the ground. Luitpold Arena would be turned 90 degrees so the grandstand faced the Great Road, eliminating the Hall of Honour and Luitpold Hall.

Speer's December 1934 plan.

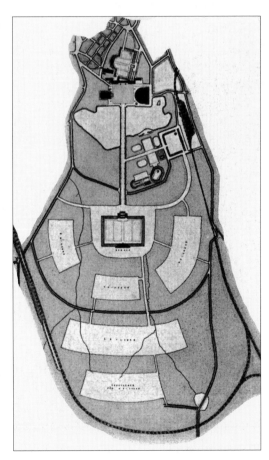

Most of the work involved a new network of wide avenues linking Luitpold Arena to the city, making it easier for columns of men to march from the Rally Grounds to the centre. Speer's plan required the demolition of many buildings and the synagogue in Hans-Sachs-Platz was one of them. His roads led to existing underpasses under the elevated railway line that cuts across the south side of the city centre and they met at Marienplatz, a new square outside the medieval city walls. A purpose-built marching route followed Lorenzer Straße to Adolf-Hitler Platz. None of these plans were implemented because of the war effort.

AN ANALYSIS OF SPEER'S PLANS

Speer portrayed himself as the driving force behind the Rally Grounds in his postwar memoirs, but this was far from the truth. Work on the Luitpold Arena was well underway when he became involved and his late plans to change its orientation never got off the drawing board. His plans to extend the Zeppelin Field were thwarted, while work on the Mars Field and the German Stadium was stopped by the war. The Congress Hall was dealt with by the Ruffs, Ludwig and Franz, while none of the buildings Speer planned to build alongside were started. The only completed elements of Speer's plans were the Great Road, the rail connections and the Langwasser campsite.

Speer's planning contribution was demonstrably reactive, some of it of his own making and some of it due to Hitler's interference. In his defence, he had to adapt his plans to accommodate the rapid increase in visitors. Speer was not the decisive architect required for a project as large as the Rally Grounds; instead he fumbled his way forward, pandering to Hitler's desires and continued to work on his pet project even when it was clear that it would never be finished. For Speer, pleasing the Führer was the only way forward.

While the Rally Grounds were no doubt a huge construction project, and one terminated before it was finished, would they have been a memorable one from an architectural point of view? Several constraints made Speer's work difficult. Having Hitler, a man who had no concept of engineering restrictions, as the client was the first. The Führer rarely took no for an answer and Speer was his yes man when it came to architecture. The need to hold the annual rally on what was essentially a construction site for the rest of the year caused many problems. Work carried out on existing structures, some of which had symbolic connections with previous rallies, had to be completed in stages. The lack of funding and time prevented demolition and rebuilding and the answer was to use time saving construction methods. The reliance on a mainly unskilled workforce did not always produce the best results.

The mixture of converted and new structures gave the Rally Grounds a random layout, in contrast to the usual solid and symmetrical designs associated with the Nazis. While new structures were built parallel or perpendicular to the Great Road, the existing ones were at a variety of angles. When Speer unveiled his architectural model of the Rally Grounds at the World Exhibition in Paris in 1937, everyone could see its haphazard nature.

Looking south across the Rally Grounds at the random nature of the layout.

The Great Road defined the layout orientation and while the Mars Field is at a right angle to the south end, Luitpold Arena sits uncomfortably at an angle at the north end. Speer planned a triumphal arch over the Great Road to obscure the unsightly dogleg into the arena. The Zeppelin Field is also at an odd angle while the Hitler Youth Stadium stands on its own.

In summary, the Nuremberg Rally Grounds were an uncomfortable mixture of old and new structures. The layout evolved to accommodate the increasing number of visitors while changes imposed by Hitler and Speer only added to the random nature of the layout. While it could be argued that Speer's vision was immense, it was never integral and never completed.

3

THE ORIGINAL STRUCTURES

While Albert Speer will always be associated with the Rally Grounds, to begin with the Nazis staged their parades in existing arenas around the Dutzendteich Lakes. Nuremberg city council and its mayor, Hermann Luppe, resisted all changes and opponents to the NSDAP resented their use of the arena. When the Nazis seized control of the city council in March 1933, all red tape and opposition disappeared under the new mayor, Willy Liebel. The NSDAP-controlled council then helped transform areas such as Luitpold Grove and the Zeppelin Arena into parade grounds.

What follows is the story behind each of the structures built before 1933. What its original purpose was and how it was changed to suit the rallies.

LUITPOLD GROVE AND LUITPOLD HALL

In 1906 a park opened on the southeast edge of Nuremberg to honour of the centenary of the city's acceptance into the Kingdom of Bavaria during the Napoleonic Wars. Luitpoldhain, or Luitpold Grove, was named after Luitpold, the Prince Regent of Bavaria. The 84,000m² park was surrounded by trees and shrubs while the centrepiece was a fountain supplied by a pumping station and water tower.

Architect Herr Härter designed an open plan steel-frame exhibition hall with plenty of windows to let in natural light, as was the fashion of the day. The building was 180 metres long, 50 metres wide and 18 metres high, and it was used for many other exhibitions, events and conferences before the First World War.

Following the Armistice, Nuremberg wanted a War Memorial to remember the 9855 soldiers from the city who had lost their lives fighting in the trenches. Rather than erect a memorial in the city centre, the decision was taken to build one in Luitpold Grove where families and friends could remember their loved ones in peaceful surroundings. After several years of discussions the Nuremberg architect Fritz Mayer was commissioned to design the Hall of Honour (*Ehrenhall*).

Luitpold Arena before Luitpold Hall in the top left corner was converted.

Mayer designed a simple rectangular building with a covered walkway facing the park where families could leave wreaths. Stone reliefs and an eternal flame completed the sombre look. The memorial was surrounded by trees and looked out onto a rectangular courtyard flanked by seven short columns. Wide paths bordered a large lawn, allowing visitors to walk from the memorial to the fountain in the centre of the park. The Hall of Honour also had two rooms containing Nuremberg's rolls of honour and the histories of the units the fallen had served in. The names of Nuremberg regiments and the places where they had served were carved on the walls. The design was accepted and the building was inaugurated in 1930.

LUITPOLD ARENA UNDER THE NAZIS

Not long after Hitler was appointed Chancellor on 30 January 1933, the decision was taken to hold the annual Party rally at Nuremberg. The Nazis seized control of the city

Hitler's vision for Luitpold Arena realised.

council in March, so for the first time there would be no objections to changing Luitpold Grove from a leisure area into a parade ground. Financing the changes would not be a problem either.

During a meeting on 21 July 1933 in Bayreuth, Hitler explained his plans for what would be known as Luitpold Arena in future. His sketches were turned into working drawings by the architect Julius Schulte-Frohlinde and the project was coordinated by the city's planning officer Walter Brugmann. The work called for a huge, level parade ground surrounded by terraces for spectators. A large grandstand called the Tribune of Honour (*Ehrentribüne*) would fill the west side. Senior Party officials would stand on the first level of the 150-metre long crescent-shaped grandstand while standard bearers stood on the second level and to each side. Three huge swastika flags flying over the centre and six-metre-high eagles at each end would complete the look. The speaker's podium faced the Hall of Honour across a wide, granite-flagged avenue, 240 metres long and 18 metres wide; another flagged path ran around the perimeter of the arena.

Hitler announced his plans only six weeks before the 1933 rally and there was no time to build a permanent structure. However, Nuremberg City Council contractors had time to level the parade ground and they worked around the clock to clear the park under the direction of the City's Parks Director, Alfred Hensel. Around 500 mature trees were cut down, hundreds of metres of hedges were uprooted and dozens of large flower beds were dug up. The area was then levelled and the earth was used to create terraces around the

The Tribune of Honour was flanked by grassy terraces.

edge of the arena. The contactors also removed the fountain and demolished the water tower and pumping station.

While the area was being cleared, a huge timber grandstand was built where the Tribune of Honour would eventually stand. The pulpit-style speakers' box was large enough for the speaker and several other officials and a two-tier grandstand stood behind. Earth terraces stretched out either side of the Tribune of Honour. Three huge 24-metre high swastika flags completed the main grandstand. They were made from perforated material and stretched between steel poles to stop them blowing in the wind.

Hitler wanted director Leni Riefenstahl to make a film of the rally but she only agreed a few days before it began. While podiums for the film crews were built in front of the grandstand, they limited the shots the cameras could make.

Despite the temporary nature of the grandstands, Luitpold Arena served its purpose during the 1933 rally. One of the highlights was when 150,000 members of the SS and the SA paraded on the grassy arena watched by 50,000 spectators. The climax of the parade was the remembrance ceremony, when Hitler and Ernst Röhm walked from the podium across to the Hall of Honour.

Work began on the permanent structures as soon as the rally finished and Albert Speer took over the design of the main grandstand. The wooden grandstand was demolished and the Tribune of Honour was built from brickwork and clad with thin granite slabs, a cheap and quick way of creating the classical look favoured by Speer and Schulte-Frohlinde.

The Hall of Honour was turned from a war memorial into a Nazi shrine.

Long, curving stone terraces stretched out along the top of the embankment. The two six-metre-high bronze eagles designed by the Munich sculptor Kurt Schmid-Ehmen were added at each end. Three seven-metre-high female figures sculptured by Josef Thorak were also added behind the Hall of Honour. The theme was the 'Victory of Work', the left-hand figure represented physical work and the right-hand figure symbolised spiritual work.

Work also continued on improving the parade ground and the central paved strip and a perimeter strip were completed in time for the 1934 rally. Paving and permanent seating was also installed on the embankments. Luitpold Arena was completed in time for the 1937 rally.

LUITPOLD HALL UNDER THE NAZIS

During the July 1933 meeting in Bayreuth, Hitler made it clear that he wanted to use Luitpold Hall as the Nazi Party conference centre. Around 16,000 delegates could gather to listen to speeches by senior Party officials in a controlled environment that was not at the mercy of the weather. However, Hitler was not happy with the turn-of-the-century look of the steel and glass exhibition hall. He eventually wanted a new, imposing structure but Luitpold Hall would have to suffice until a new hall was built.

Although it would have been relatively simple to demolish Luitpold Hall, it would have been impossible to rebuild a new one in the twelve-month period between rallies. Instead, Albert Speer was commissioned to change the external look of the building while Benno von Arent's stage designers were commissioned to dress up the interior.

Luitpold Hall after Speer
added the concrete façades
at each end.

Speer designed two huge edifices, one for each end of the building, hiding the glass and steel frontage behind an imposing granite edifice; or at least a brick edifice clad in thin granite slabs. The main entrance faced the south-west corner of the Luitpold Arena and steps led up to the entrance where three high doors allowed standard bearers to carry their flags inside. Adolf Hitler's personal banner, the *Fahnentuch*, adorned the centre of the flat granite wall above. Ten enormous swastika flags hung down either side of the doors, breaking up the bleak aspect of the edifice. Lights were also installed to illuminate the façade at night.

Luitpold Hall had been designed as an exhibition hall, where people could inspect displays. It had a large, open central nave and while two parallel rows of steel columns supported the roof, large glass windows let in natural light. Although Hitler did not like the building, it was the largest available in the city and it was next to the Luitpold Arena. However, it had not been designed for 16,000 people to cram inside for several hours and the change of use would cause problems, particularly on a warm autumn afternoon.

SA standard bearers parade in front of the Luitpold Hall.

With only six weeks to prepare for the September rally, Benno von Arent's stage design-ers created the maximum visual impact in the limited time available. They used huge sheets of fabric to hide the steel structure, transforming the interior into an austere cathedral-like space. White fabric was hung in front of the windows, so daylight would still illuminate the hall. Large strips of fabric hung from the ceiling and while they hid the roof structure, air could still circulate. Black fabric was also pinned around the supporting columns and decorated with an eagle and swastika emblem. Arent dressed the temporary stage with fab-rics and pine branches to complete the look. New wiring was also installed so the building interior, or rather the 'tent' interior, could be illuminated.

Music was important for controlling the momentum of the meeting and while fanfares announced the start of the meeting, quieter pieces filled the interludes. Songs, like the national anthem and *Horst Wesel Lied*, the Party anthem, were part of the spectacle. A large brass and string band was seated behind the Party officials and a huge organ was installed to underpin their efforts.

While Luitpold Hall had been designed to create optical and acoustic effects that reflected the Party's political ideas, the designers had overlooked one important factor; body heat. They had concentrated on the look rather than the practicalities and had forgotten to provide sufficient ventilation. When 16,000 people crammed into the hall and the sun hit the windows, the temperature rose to unbearable levels. The fabric prevented air circulating while the dozens of spotlights increased the temperature in the airless room. Many would feel faint as they sat listening to the long speeches. After two years Albert Speer's team took note and new air conditioning and permanent lighting fixtures were installed in time for the 1935 rally.

Although work had started on a new Congress Hall only a short distance away, Hitler impatiently suggested new ideas. Speer turned the ideas into workable plans and the contractors were put to work building them. Although many features involved making difficult alterations to the existing structure, money was no object.

As late as 1938, Benno von Arent was commissioned to redesign Luitpold Hall, even though work on the new Congress Hall was well on its way. His plans were never implemented because the 1939 rally was cancelled and work on the Rally Grounds stopped the following year.

Luitpold Hall's interior was dressed with fabrics, creating an 'airless tent'.

THE NUREMBERG ZOO

The area south of Luitpold Arena and west of the Congress Hall had been a zoo for many years when the Nazis decided to develop the area. The area had animal cages, four ponds for wild birds and an artificial mountain for mountain goats. The animal zones were also surrounded by public leisure areas.

It all changed in 1933 when the animals were taken away and the cages were removed to make way for construction materials for the Congress Hall; all that remained were the ponds. Three years later a 1:1 scale wooden model of part of the Congress Hall, around 58 metres wide and 60 metres high, was built on the area. Speer's plan to build a Hall of Culture on the site never materialised.

THE ZEPPELIN FIELD

One of the first airships to fly over Germany landed south east of the Dutzendteich Lakes in 1909 and the name Zeppelin Field stuck. Following the First World War the area was turned into an outdoor arena measuring 378 by 362 metres, surrounded by earth embankments for spectators. It was used for sporting events and political rallies.

The Rally organisers starting planning how to get the most from the arena as soon the Nazis seized control of Nuremberg City Council in March 1933. They only had six months before the next rally so they again erected temporary timber structures. A large wooden grandstand with a speaker's podium, solid sides and open railings was built on the east terrace. A large eagle fashioned out of timber planks was built above the grandstand and three huge swastika flags flew at each end. While the organisers had created a functional solution in time for the September Rally, the image was temporary and unimpressive; the opposite of what the Nazi leaders wanted to portray.

When Albert Speer became involved in the Rally Grounds in April 1934, he drew up designs to improve the Zeppelin Field. His first plan was to triple the length of the arena along the south bank of Dutzendteich Lake, so it could accommodate larger military manoeuvres. However, the poor ground and a high water table meant that the work could never be completed between rallies.

Instead, Speer chose a new location as part of his grand design for the Party Rally Grounds published in December 1934. The collosal new arena for war games would be built at the south end of the Grounds and it would be called the Mars Field. In the meantime Speer planned a simple redesign to create a permanent image for the Zeppelin Field.

An impressive new grandstand would be built on the eastern embankment, while the rest of the earth embankments would be upgraded with steps for spectators. Speer drew his inspiration for a classical design from the Pergamon Altar, built during the reign of King Eumenes II in the first half of the second century BC. The altar had been built on one of the terraces of the Acropolis in the ancient city of Pergamon in Asia Minor. Archaeologists dismantled the structure and it was taken to Germany where it had been on display in Berlin's Pergamon Museum since 1930. The structure had a 20-metre-wide flight of stairs

The SA gather in front of the Zeppelin Arena's temporary grandstand.

climbing to an altar platform 35 metres wide and 33 metres deep. A long colonnade and high relief friezes completed the structure.

Speer planned a similar style structure for the Zeppelin Field grandstand, only his design was far bigger. Hitler and other leaders would stand on a large speaker's podium in the centre, surrounded by senior Party officials, while delegates could sit or stand on the terraces. A long colonnade dressed with huge swastika flags would form a backdrop while Party leaders would gather in a hall behind the speaker's podium.

Cosmetic work would also be carried out on the remaining seven-metre-high embankments, giving them a permanent look. Stone-faced terraces would be added on the inner sides while entrance steps were added on the outer faces. Walls at the top of the embankments regulated the 70,000 spectators as they took their places on the terraces.

Thirty-four stone-clad rectangular towers would be built at regular intervals on the outside of the embankments, around the perimeter of the arena. Each one had six tall flag poles on top, so 204 large swastika flags could be flown around the sides. Once completed,

The completed Zeppelin Tribune.

the Zeppelin Field would resemble a castle from the outside, with its earth wall, stone turrets and flags.

There were three wide entrances to the Zeppelin Arena. The two on the north and south sides of the perimeter would be connected by a 50-metre-wide asphalt road running in front of the main grandstand. Vehicles would drive and men would march along the road, right in front of the speaker's podium. The official report of the Reich Party Congress 1936 explained how Hitler 'did not see the men, but one saw a grey mass…'

The third entrance was on the west side of the Zeppelin Arena, facing the speaker's podium. After their march past, troops would re-enter the arena and deploy while the parade continued. A new road would eventually be built through the woods, connecting the west entrance to the rest of the Rally Grounds.

Work started on the Zeppelin Field as soon as the 1934 rally finished but time was a problem. Speer knew what effect he was looking for but the grandstand would have to be built in stages. By the time of the 1935 rally, the steps and the speaker's podium were ready; work on the terraces was also completed. A huge eagle with its feet gripping a swastika was still above the grandstand, only this time it was a far more professional structure supported by eight flagpoles.

Although the grandstand looked as it if was built from solid granite, this was an illusion. It was another brickwork structure covered in granite cladding; a short cut to create a classic architectural look. Although Speer aimed to build structures that would last for hundreds of years, he failed when it came to the Zeppelin Field grandstand. The stone was quarried from over 30 different quarries, and the different shades and grains spoiled the overall monolithic effect he desired.

The building work was also rushed to get the grandstand ready in time for the 1935 rally and mistakes were made. Many stone slabs were stacked directly on the ground rather than on pallets during the cold winter months and some suffered frost damage. Poor quality control meant that the damaged slabs were used and it detracted from the overall image. Some observers even dared to make negative comments. The problem was never solved and the stone continues to crumble despite remedial measures taken in the 1980s.

As soon as the September 1935 rally ended, the builders returned to concentrate on the colonnade that formed the backdrop to Speer's spectacle. An assembly hall was built in the centre, behind the speaker's podium. Senior Party officials would be driven to ground-floor doors at the rear and then climb internal stairs into the assembly hall. While they waited to take their place on the grandstand, they would have gazed at Hermann Kaspar's mosaics of interlocking swastikas on the ceiling. At the specified time the doors opened and the officials took their places on the terraces all together. Hitler was the last to enter just before the parade was about to begin.

Seventy-two rectangular pillars stood either side of the assembly hall and they were connected by a plain entablature (a horizontal connecting beam across the top). The colonnade was 20 metres high and huge swastika flags hung between the pillars, doing away with the need for standard bearers to parade along the top of the steps. Buttresses closed off the ends of the colonnade and they were adorned with bronze swastikas and wreaths sculptured by Arno Breker. Large cauldrons filled with flaming oil placed at either end completed the spectacle.

Searchlights illuminate the Zeppelin Tribune.

The Zeppelin Arena terraces with their buttresses.

Following the 1936 rally a large gilded swastika was built on the roof of the assembly hall, completing the Zeppelin Field. Speer created what became known as the 'Light Dome' or 'Cathedral of Light', to show off his work at the 1937 rally. He used dozens of searchlights to illuminate the night sky and the white columns of the colonnade.

Despite Speer's plan to move the Wehrmacht's war games to the larger Mars Field, the new arena was never completed and the Zeppelin Field was used again in 1938.

THE FRANKEN STADIUM

In the 1920s Mayor Hermann Luppe was responsible for promoting an extensive outdoor sports and leisure complex in the woods south of Dutzendteich Lakes. The area was planned by the City Parks Director Alfred Hensel and it was awarded a gold medal in the 1928 Amsterdam Olympiad Architecture Competition. It was also considered to be a political success for Mayor Luppe.

While the complex had an outdoor swimming pool, the sports stadium became an integral part of the Rally Grounds. It was designed by Otto Ernst Schweizer and had an international design rather than the style favoured by German architects at the time. It was built between 1926 and 1928 and when finished, it was considered one of the best modern structures of the Weimar Republic.

The Hitler Youth gather in the Franken Stadium.

The arena had a rectangular sports field in the centre with a classic oval shape running track around the perimeter. The main stand was covered by a flat, cantilevered canopy while the rest of the stands were open to the elements. Around 50,000 people could fit into the stadium if many paraded on the sports field.

Schweizer's design proved to be just what the Nazis wanted for their Day of the Hitler Youth. The initial alterations were minor. A timber stage was built for the Party leaders under the stadium canopy and timber towers for drummers and trumpeters were added around the stadium. The stadium entrances were widened at a later stage to reduce the crush before and after the parade.

On the Day of the Hitler Youth around 50,000 boys of the Hitler Youth and 5000 girls of the German Girls League gathered in the stadium to listen to their Führer and their leader, Baldur von Schirach.

4

THE NEW STRUCTURES

The first major addition to the Rally Grounds was a new Congress Hall on the banks of Dutzendteich Lake, a large, solid structure to replace the aging Luitpold Hall. It was designed by local architect Ludwig Ruff and supervised by his son Franz following his untimely death.

Speer had created a pleasing backdrop with huge swastikas for the 1933 May Day celebrations in Berlin and when he began work on designs for the 1933 Nuremberg Rally, Hitler asked him to do the same there. Yet again Speer's simple, yet effective, designs made an impact on the Führer and he was appointed 'Commissioner for the Artistic and Technical Presentation of Party Rallies and Demonstrations'.

Following Paul Troost's death in March 1934, Speer was appointed the Party's chief architect and head of the Chief Office of Construction. He was soon involved with the Rally Grounds and following the September rally, produced two layout designs detailing several new structures.

What follows is the story behind each of the structures built after 1933 from concept to completion or to some kind of conclusion; some never got off the drawing board.

THE CONGRESS HALL

In 1931 Nuremberg architect Ludwig Ruff was asked to draw up plans for a new city hall to be built on the side of Dutzendteich Lake. His design was for a horseshoe-shaped building with the entrance vestibule facing out across the water so that night lighting would provide an impressive reflection of the edifice. Although the plans were published in the press, arguments between Ruff and Mayor Hermann Luppe meant that the project was still under negotiation when the Nazis seized power.

The Nazis replaced Luppe with Mayor Willy Liebel in March 1933 and their decision to use the Dutzendteich area for their annual rally meant that Ruff's design had a future. At the end of the year Hitler instructed Ludwig Ruff to build a 'modern amphitheatre' to replace the Luitpold Hall. While the old hall was being converted to act as the rally's

Ludwig Ruff's design for the Congress Hall's main entrance.

The Coliseum-style colonnade where the delegates entered the Congress Hall.

indoor meeting hall, it could only seat 16,000 people. Hitler wanted a new Congress Hall capable of seating 50,000.

The new project was much larger than the city hall and while Ruff had to completely rework his plans he did keep some of the same design elements, including the overall shape and elevations. Hitler was pleased with the neo-Hellenic designs when he saw them in June 1934 and he increased the budget stating that it would be 'really great and monumental for all time'.

Ruff referred to the new structure as the Congress Building but many called it the Coliseum, because of its colonnade design, even though its design was more like a Roman theatre than an amphitheatre. It was also 1.7 times higher and 1.3 times longer than Rome's Coliseum. The building would measure 275 metres long by 265 metres wide.

Ruff choose granite for the façade to make the structure imposing and dominating, like the structures of ancient Rome. While granite was long-lasting and durable, it was only for show. The structure was going to be built out of brick and concrete and clad in thin granite slabs to save money and time.

Ruff's horseshoe plan had senior Party officials entering via the main entrance on the straight side of the structure while delegates entering via the curved colonnade. In Speer's original plan the main entrance faced south but in his December 1934 plan the building had been turned through 90 degrees, so the main entrance faced east across the lake. This made the curved side of the structure face the plaza at the top of the Great Road, creating plenty of space for delegates to gather before and after meetings.

The main entrance was an open-plan colonnade with a massive eagle carved into the wall above. Rectangular vestibules, 57 metres long and 24 metres wide, stood either side of the entrance, closing off the ends of the colonnade. Officials would walk through the entrance vestibule and enter the hall, taking their seat behind the speaker's podium. Delegates passed through the arches in the 435 metre long colonnade and entered the hall through one of the triple door entrances on the first or second floor.

The huge internal area was approximately 180 metres long and 160 metres wide. It was 68.5 metres high and illuminated by a large fanlight glass window in the roof. Ruff's design had no supporting columns, creating a vast open space where all the delegates could see the Party leaders. The pulpit-like speaker's podium and the organ with its 16,013 pipes would give meetings a religious air. When the organ was first ordered from the long-established firm of Walckers, Franz Adam, conductor of the Reich Symphony Orchestra, set down a number of pre-requisites, one of which was that the immense range of the organ should not attract the attention of individual listeners 'because of artistic subtleties but must rather bring out the spirit of the Party'.

Ludwig Ruff died unexpectedly in August 1934 and he only saw the early excavations of the largest building of his career. Instead his inexperienced son Franz had to take up where his father had left off and carry on with one of the Nazis' largest construction projects. He had been given an impossible task, having to oversee a complex project for difficult clients who would not take no for an answer.

Hitler, Mayor Willy Liebel and Franz Ruff attended the groundbreaking ceremony in 1935 where the Führer announced that the Party elite would gather inside the hall every

The footprint of the
Congress Hall marked
out next to the
Dutzendteich Lakes.

year for centuries to come. He also made it clear that if the Nazi Party ever came to an end, people would be still talking about buildings like the Congress Hall for decades to come.

While Ruff's new design was what Hitler wanted to see, the time had come to find out if it could be built. Engineers from Hochtief, Philipp Holzmann and Siemens Bauunion, were appointed to study different elements of the building and they then worked together to come up with solutions. With time pressing, work began on the foundations.

The building stood next to Dutzendteich Lake and it appears that little thought had been given to the water table. Water began seeping into the excavation and it was pouring in by the time the required level was reached. The management team decided to install a compacted layer of sand and granite chippings around the excavation. A watertight seal was eventually formed around the massive excavation and although it had been an expensive solution, money was no object. Work on the three-metre-thick foundation slab then started as the first of thousands of tonnes of concrete began to be poured into the hole.

Meanwhile, Ruff was dealing with the numerous changes imposed upon him, many of them by Hitler, a man who believed he had the vision for great architecture even though he had no qualifications or experience. The main change to the hall was the increase in height from 40 to 60 metres and while the extra height imposed new, and perhaps impossible, structural challenges, Ruff did not say no to the Führer and Speer.

The technical difficulties meant that there would be nothing to see apart from a huge hole until the 1938 rally but organisers wanted visitors to see how grandiose their scheme

Visitors admire the model of the Congress Hall.

was; and they wanted to show them quickly. Two wooden 1:1 scale models, one external and one interior, were built next to the building site. The outer segment had seven ground level arches and it demonstrated how the two upper floors and the roof construction would look. The interior segment illustrated how the 17-metre-high seating and the colonnade above worked together.

Two dozen tower cranes appeared on the skyline in 1938 and when visitors returned to the September rally they saw the beginnings of the semi-circular brick and concrete carcasse with its granite cladding. The cancellation of the 1939 rally meant that they did not come back to see the Congress Hall.

As work on the walls got underway, discussions about the roof began in earnest in 1938. Ruff's design for a huge open space was what the Nazis wanted but a roof span as large as the Congress Hall had never been built before. The roof would have to cantilever out over the 180 x 160 metres space, meeting up around the large arch-shaped window. Over the next two years the designers struggled with a practical solution but the arguments were still unresolved by the time work was being wound down.

The main entrance vestibule was supported by marble columns and they stood between two halls. Although the halls had been included in Ruff's initial design, no definite plans for their use were determined until late on. Following the annexation of Austria in March 1938 the Nazis planned to move the Imperial Regalia from Vienna to Nuremberg and they intended to display them in the south wing. The decision was taken to house the Congress Hall staff in the north wing and plans to install offices, mess rooms and storage facilities were in progress when work stopped.

As building work progressed, a new model of the interior, this time at a scale of 1:10, was built in time for the 1938 rally and it was electrically illuminated to show the Führer what the finished Hall would look like. As soon as the building was high enough, the interior model was moved inside and hung from concrete brackets cast into the brick walls. Additional brackets were added and a variety of marble test panels were hung on them so everyone could see which one was the best.

Germany invaded Poland in the very week that the 1939 Rally was scheduled to take place and construction soon ground to a halt as workers were conscripted into the armed forces. The project was never formally cancelled and work continued slowly throughout 1940 and 1941 while stone facing slabs were still being delivered in 1942. The incomplete building suffered damage during the many Allied bombing raids and Soviet prisoners of war were drafted in to carry out repairs in 1942 and 1943; many of them were later executed.

While the estimated costs for the Congress Hall were around 15 million Reichmarks in 1934, they had risen to around 65 million Reichsmarks by 1935; some estimate that they may have risen to over 80 million. As the overall budget for the Rally Grounds was over 280 million marks, it meant that the Congress Hall absorbed 25 per cent of the total. While the German Stadium was a much larger structure, it never went past the initial construction preparation stage.

By the end of war the Congress Hall was an incomplete shell rather than the imposing edifice the Nazis had wanted, like so many of Hitler's and Speer's plans. The walls were still

Work on the Zeppelin Tribune continues at full speed.

20 metres below their planned height while the designers had never found a solution to the cantilevered roof; we will never know if the roof could have been built.

THE GREAT ROAD

As early as December 1934 Albert Speer's plans included the Great Road, a wide paved area cutting through the centre of the Rally Grounds. The alignment of the Great Road was significant because it was set to run from the Mars Field to the Luitpold Arena, aiming in the direction the Imperial Castle in the heart of the old city. Troops marching north along the road would have seen the castle on the horizon, symbolically linking the medieval empire with the Third Reich. Troops marching south would have seen the commanders of the armed forces on the Mars Field main grandstand.

Speer was still tinkering with his layout in 1940 and he planned to turn Luitpold Arena through 90 degrees so that the main grandstand looked down the Great Road; that plan never got off the drawing board. The Great Road was to be the central axis of the Rally Ground, making an ideal parade ground for the Wehrmacht and the Party organisations. The Zeppelin Field had always been considered too small.

The Great Road connected Luitpold Arena and the Congress Hall to the new Mars Field. It ran straight past the site of the German Stadium where a staircase led up to the entrance atrium; opposite would be a platform for Hitler and his guests of honour. A narrower side road through the forest connected the Zeppelin Field to the Great Road.

At two kilometres long and 60 metres wide, the road was by far the most destructive of Speer's structures. Parts of the Dutzendteich Lakes had to be filled in so the road could pass between them while large parts of the forest were felled along the route. Construction work started in 1935 and it took four years to complete because the marshy ground around the lakes had to be drained before construction work began.

Around 120,000 square metres of square granite slabs (around 100,000 slabs) then had to be laid in perfect alignment and level. The slabs had an abrasive upper surface for grip and the joints were filled with a darker coloured mortar, creating a grid of parallel lines which the soldiers could follow as they marched along the monotonous expanse.

Slabs stockpiled in front of the Congress Hall.

Dutzendteich Lakes had to be remodelled to make way for the Great Road.

Troops never marched down the road past the German Stadium as intended because the September 1939 rally was cancelled. As previously mentioned, instead of marching through Nuremberg, the Wehrmacht were marching into Poland.

Despite all the work lavished on the Great Road, the plaza-style area at the north end typifies the disorganised planning that plagued the Rally Grounds. Speer's original plan ignored the area but his December 1934 plan had the Great Road ending in an unresolved area in front of the Congress Hall. The problem was that the Luitpold Arena was out of alignment with the Great Road and its main grandstand faced east rather than south. Speer intended to build a Triumphal Arch and an Exhibition Hall at the entrance to the Luitpold Arena, creating the illusion that everything was in alignment; they were never built.

A Hall of Culture would have been built on the west side of the plaza, where the Nuremberg Zoo once stood, and it looked out on two large obelisks either side of the Great Road. Neither the buildings nor the pillars were built.

THE GERMAN STADIUM

Speer's 1935 plan for the Rally Grounds included a huge open air stadium on the west side of the Great Road, close to the midpoint. Speer was determined not to disappoint Hitler in his passion for huge architecture and he designed what would be the largest open air stadium in the world, one capable of holding 400,000 spectators; the population of Nuremberg in 1934.

Albert Speer's model for the German Stadium.

The horseshoe-shaped structure would measure 600 by 440 metres, about four times larger than the Congress Hall, and it would fill the space between the Great Road and Münchener Straße. At 120 metres high, the stadium would be higher than the spire of St Lorenz Church's in the centre of Nuremberg and larger than Rome's Circus Maximus arena.

Hitler also had definite plans about what would happen in the 380- by 150-metre arena. Although the 1940 Olympic Games had been awarded to Tokyo, he planned to turn Nuremberg into the home of the Olympiad and hold all future Games in the German Stadium. There were also plans to replace the traditional field and track athletics with new military-themed events.

Sample competitions were held during the 1937 and 1938 rallies to judge their reception by the crowds and the pentathlon-style events had twelve-man teams competing in their uniforms and carrying knapsacks. The crowds watched the competitors complete a 250m obstacle course, shoot small-calibre weapons, throw grenades and then participate in a 20km route march.

Everything was being planned on a massive scale; the bowls that held the burning oil to light up the platform area would be six metres in diameter. The cost of the project was also going to be huge but Hitler refused to talk about the finances. Instead he reminded the doubters that Fredrick the Great had not questioned how much was being spent on the Sanssouci Palace (from the French for 'carefree'), when it was being built in Potsdam, Berlin, in the eighteenth century.

The Great Road ran straight past the open end of the German Stadium and Speer's plan included a wide staircase leading up from the pavement. A long colonnade with 22 columns stood at the top of the steps and they opened into a rectangular entrance court-yard measuring 260 metres by 120 metres. The courtyard had colonnades on two sides and Speer's design meant that people would not see the scale of stadium until they had passed through the entrance hall, increasing the visual impact.

On 9 July 1937 the cornerstone for the new German Stadium was laid and the south west of the Dutzendteich Lakes became a hive of activity as forestry teams cleared the trees and construction teams levelled the ground ready for the excavations. Before long there were over 1500 men working on the site, controlled by two management teams. While engineers from Heillmann and Littmann, Dykerhoff and Widmann, Grün and Bilfinger, Stöhr and Boswau and Knauer supervised the north side of the project, engineers from Hochtief, Siemens Bauunion, Philipp Holzmann and Deutsche Bauunion looked after the south side.

Although visitors to Nuremberg could visit the 1:1 scale models of the nearby Congress Hall, there would be no model of the German Stadium. It was too big. All that was on offer were Speer's architectural models and it took a lot of imagination to grasp what was going to be built.

Early in 1938 work started on specimen sections of the structure so that Speer could prepare design sections ready to show Hitler. Two masonry pillars were built and clad with granite to check the aesthetics.

Speer also wanted two 1:1 models of the terraces to be built at different angles to make sure the crowds could see the arena from every level. Their view of the arena would be obscured if the slope of the seating was too shallow. They might suffer from vertigo or nausea if the slope was too steep.

The Hirschbachtal valley, near Oberklausen, 20 miles north east of Nuremberg, was chosen because the gradient of the valley sides almost matched that of the stadium. While Hitler was not interested in the cost of the stadium, Speer kept the cost of the models to a minimum and concrete bases supported a timber superstructure representing the seating. Both models were complete in time for Hitler's visit in March 1938.

Two models of the terracing were built at different angles in Hirschbachtal valley.

The SS used slave labourers to quarry the granite.

While work continued on the huge foundations, Speer was looking at the designs of the final structure and a large model of a stairway was delivered to the site in 1939. Hitler was interested in progress on the stadium and always eager to see the models but it would take Speer another 12 months to complete the plans, by which time Germany was at war. Before work stopped, Hitler approved the choice of granite, using a red stone for the outer façade and white stone for the interior seating. It meant that planning for the procurement of thousands of tonnes of granite could begin.

By the time the quarrying contracts were awarded to the SS-controlled German Earth & Stone Works Company, or D.E.S.T. for short (*Deutsche Erd und Steinwerke GmbH*), Germany had invaded Poland. The SS had acquired mineral deposits and they opened new concentration camps ready to supply slave labourers for the quarries.

The Flossenbürg concentration camp had been opened in the Oberpfalz region of Bavaria, Germany, in May 1938 and the white granite had already been used on several structures on the Rally Grounds. With building work imminent on the German Stadium, orders for large quantities of granite were placed but there were problems. Slave labour was in short supply and the war effort came first. Many construction workers had already been conscripted and while 1000 concentration camp prisoners were moved to Nuremberg to work on the stadium, work was seriously disrupted.

Deliveries continued from Flossenbürg quarries while extra stone came from Mauthausen (upper Austria) and Groß-Rosen (lower Silesia) concentration camps. Natzweiler concentration camp was also opened in the Vosges region of France in 1941, next to a new quarry chosen for its reddish coloured granite.

Despite efforts by the management teams to keep the project moving forward, the disruption caused by the war meant that work never started on the superstructure. Speer was not put off by the lack of progress and he continued to tinker with the design, causing problems for the engineers, until he finally lost interest in 1942.

As staff and labourers left the site to join their military units, work ground to a halt. Hitler and Speer had forgotten about the project and a large horseshoe-shaped hole filled with water was all that was left. The tiny foundation stone was the only permanent reminder that the hole was the foundation for the 'largest stadium in the world'.

THE MARS FIELD

The 'Day of the Armed Forces' was the last day of the annual rally and for many it was the highlight of the week. Compared to the endless parades, marching and speeches, the sight of tanks and artillery pieces battling alongside infantry while the Luftwaffe's planes flew overhead was an exciting spectacle. The Nazi leaders and the Wehrmacht generals wanted to increase the scale and complexity of the wargames but the Zeppelin Field was too small to accommodate their plans. A larger battleground was needed.

Speer's original plan was to increase the Zeppelin Field to three times its size but after learning that the ground had been a problem when the original structure was built, a new plan had to be made. While money was no object it would have been impossible to complete the extension in time for the next annual rally.

The acquisition of the large area of woodland to the south of the Dutzendteich Lake allowed Speer to submit a bold new design for an enlarged Rally Grounds in December 1934. The Zeppelin Field would stay the same size and a huge new arena would be built at the southern end of the Great Road instead. The arena would be called the Mars Field, after the Roman god of war, and it would be used for manoeuvres, military displays and wargames. The rectangular field measured 955 by 610 metres and would be developed as 'natural moor landscape' to help create realistic wargames.

The arena would be surrounded by 14-metre-high stands, seating 150,000 spectators, more than twice the number of the Zeppelin Field. Speer again planned to build columns around the perimeter and 24 would serve as staircases for the spectators. Each one would measure 16 by 13.5 metres in plan and be 38 metres high; supported by six-metre-deep foundations. There would be 24 flag poles between each tower and when complete the stadium would be surrounded by over 500 18-metre-high swastika flags stretched taut so they did not flap in the wind. An underground tunnel ran beneath the grandstands so a small train could move the flags and poles around the stadium.

A single wide entrance on the north side of the arena opened on to the Great Road. Party leaders and generals would sit in the grandstand opposite, watching as troops

The Great Road ran north from the Mars Field, passing the Great Stadium.

marched and vehicles drove into the arena. The arena was very much a larger version of the Zeppelin Field.

Work on clearing the 60 hectares (150 acres) began in 1935 and continued through the winter and into the spring. Excavation work for tower foundations was delayed until after the 1936 rally so the construction teams did not interfere with the visitors on the Langwasser campsite. Work began in earnest after the rally and there was always a minimum of 4000 workers on site; double that number were sometimes employed.

Speer planned to decorate the Mars Field with huge sculptures in the style of heroic figures. Originally he planned to erect an eagle statue behind the speaker's platform, similar to the one on the Zeppelin Field grandstand. When the sculptor Josef Thorak was appointed in 1937 the eagle was replaced by three 12-metre-high bronze figures. The goddess of victory holding a laurel was in the centre, a male sword bearer to the left and male shield bearer to the right; the three statues were flanked by men holding horses. The group represented the heroic deeds and inevitable sacrifices that were needed for victory. Thorak was also commissioned to create a pair of huge mounted figures to stand either side of the Mars Field entrance. The figure to the left carried a flag levelled over his shoulder while the one to the right carried a spear in the same position.

A 1:10 model of the group sculpture was approved by Hitler in April 1938 and Thorak was instructed to defer other work and concentrate on the Mars Field sculptures. A final model of the group, four metres high, was displayed in the House of German Art in Munich. Despite all the attention and work lavished on the bronze sculptures, interest waned following the outbreak of war. The Mars Field was never completed and the statues were never displayed.

After three years of hard work, only the western half of the Mars Field was nearing completion when work was rapidly scaled down in September 1939. Only eleven towers, part of the tunnel and sections of the western grandstands had been completed. Although work restarted following the fall of France in June 1940, it did not last for long. The incomplete structures were hidden beneath camouflage netting in an attempt to prevent them from being bombed for the rest of the war.

The Mars Field would have completed Speer's vision for the Rally Grounds.

The SS Barracks was a late addition to the Rally Grounds.

THE SS-BARRACKS

In 1936 a new building was added to Speer's plans for the Rally Grounds. A huge barracks (a *Kaserne*) for Nuremberg's SS units was to be built a short distance west of the Congress Hall. Franz Ruff was commissioned to start work on the building in 1936, with instructions to use a similar design to the Congress Hall.

The foundation stone ceremony was held in December 1936 and a number of important Nazi leaders attended, including Reichsführer-SS Heinrich Himmler, Gauleiter Julius Streicher and Mayor Willy Liebel. The architects Albert Speer, Walter Brugmann and Franz Ruff also attended.

The barracks were to be built at the junction of Frankenstraße and Münchener Straße and the footprint of the building was a controversial one. Several roads had to be closed, a tram car route had to be diverted and a large number of buildings had to be demolished. The city planners put forward objections, which Liebel contested, but when it became apparent that building works could be delayed, Himmler stepped in. He made it clear in writing that nothing must be allowed to stop progress.

The young designer Ruff once again faced the difficult situation of having to please the Nazi leaders and work with the structural engineers and the construction company. The SS had standard designs for many rooms and facilities and while this facilitated the design work, work still had not started by the time of the September 1937 rally. Hitler was infuriated by the lack of progress and he ordered digging to start immediately because the building had to be ready for the 1938 Rally.

The main building had two barrack wings each surrounding an inner courtyard while a range of auxiliary buildings to the south surrounded a large parade ground. The imposing granite entrance was in the centre of the building's north wall, facing Frankenstraße, and it had a large eagle above the archway. It did not help that the original design had to be altered to include classrooms and barracks for the SS weapons company.

The construction teams did begin straight away and while the chosen structural steel with brick and cladding design was the fastest construction method, there was no way of completing the barracks in time for the 1938 rally. The barracks was finished in the spring of 1939 and the building was celebrated as the gateway to the Rally Grounds during the opening ceremony on 2 June 1939.

While the SS units went into battle in Poland, police units were given military training here. Some would later join the SS-Einsatzgruppen death squads who rounded up and killed Jews and others in Poland and the Soviet Union. SS weapons units also had communications training in the classrooms.

In 1941 prisoners from Dachau concentration camp were moved into the barracks so they could work in factories across Nuremberg. Prisoners were later moved here from Flossenbürg concentration camp and they also were employed as slave labourers across the city, often clearing rubble from the streets following Allied air raids.

The 'Strength through Joy' town celebrated German culture.

THE STRENGTH THROUGH JOY (*KRAFT DURCHE FREUDE*) VILLAGE

In 1936 the decision was taken to stage a demonstration of German cultural life at the Berlin Olympic Games. Julius Schulte-Frohlinde designed five Folk Law Halls and they were drawn up by the German Labour Front. Each one had a regional theme; the Rhine Hall, the Hamburg Hall, the Berlin Hall, the Bavarian Hall and the Frankfurt Hall. Labour Front workmen erected the wooden exhibition halls and they were visited by thousands of people.

After the Olympic Games the decision was taken to relocate the exhibition halls to Nuremberg and a piece of land was selected on the northeast side of the Rally Grounds, across the Regensburg road from the Zeppelin Field. Labour Front workmen erected the halls, creating a festival park surrounded by woodland. The Strength through Joy Village opened in time for the September 1937 rally and the intention was to make it a permanent fixture.

The Frankfurt Hall was over three times the size of the other four halls, 80 metres long, 44 metres wide and 28 metres high. While it could hold 3500 persons the rest could accommodate 1000. Visitors were able to see examples of local architecture and clothing, and taste local food and drink. The organisers encouraged a beer tent atmosphere, holding community singing and dancing events. A bell tower in the centre of the park made sure visitors were on time for the parades and rallies.

The Strength through Joy Village was burnt to the ground during an air raid on 29 August 1942.

5

ARCHITECTS, DESIGNERS AND PLANNERS

THE ARCHITECTS

While Albert Speer came up with the overall layout of the Nuremberg Rally Grounds, he was just one of a number of architects who were involved in the design of individual structures. The Luitpold and Zeppelin Arenas were existing structures that were upgraded, as was the Luitpold Hall. The Franken Stadium, which would become associated with the Hitler Youth, was designed by Otto Schweizer. Ludwig Ruff was an established local architect who was commissioned to design the new Congress Hall and his son Franz took over following his sudden death in August 1934.

Speer was appointed the NSDAP's chief architect following Paul Troost's death in March 1934 and he immediately became involved with the Rally Grounds. His ambition and close working relationship with the Führer meant that he could propose grandiose plans, upgrade existing structures and add new ones. His December 1934 proposal also included outline plans for new infrastructure to get the crowds to Nuremberg and accommodation for them.

Otto Schweizer (1890–1965): The Franken Stadium

Schweizer came from south-west Germany and studied architecture at Stuttgart and Munich, gaining his degree in 1917. After working at the Bavarian Friedrich Krupp Gun Works in Munich, he returned home following the Armistice to join Schramberg council. After working in Stuttgart's and Schwäbisch Gmünd's planning departments, he transferred to Nuremberg in 1925. Over the next four years he worked on the Labour Office, the Planetarium and the Franken Stadium, which would be used for the Hitler Youth rallies. He also won an award for his design of the Prater Stadium in Vienna.

In 1930 Schweizer was appointed professor at Karlsruhe's Technical College and he later took the chair at Berlin-Charlottenburg Technical University. In 1937 he joined the German examination board. Following the war he joined the board advising on Germany's construction needs and the Council of Superior Architecture and Urbanism. Schweizer ended his career as a consultant in Mannheim.

Albert Speer was a master of creating theatrical backdrops.

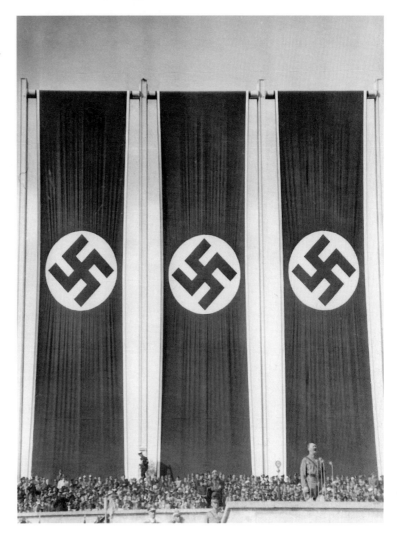

Ludwig Ruff (1878–1934)

Ruff worked for his father's building company before moving to Munich for further training. In 1903 he was conscripted into the army and became an apprentice architect with I Bavarian Corps' Quartermaster Department. Two years later he founded a private practice, Wildanger and Ruff, with offices in Regensburg and Straubing, southeast of Nuremberg.

In 1908 Ruff took part in a Nuremberg design competition and was awarded second prize for his design of the Gibitzenhof apartments in the southern suburbs. He was then employed by Maschinenfabrik Augsburg Nürnberg AG (MAN), a company employing 4000 people primarily engaged in the automotive industry.

Ruff's role was to improve the company's image in the city by designing pleasing buildings. One of his main projects was the Werderau apartments, a complex built in the southern suburbs for company employees. Building began in 1910 and it would become a major part of his life's work. He also designed the reconstruction of the city's Apollo Theatre.

Temporary structures were used while the architects finalised their plans.

Ruff continued his work after the war, designing apartment blocks, villas and small houses. He also designed several war memorials across Germany. His major project in 1927 was the Phoebus Palace Cinema, one of the largest in Germany with over 2000 seats. As one of the leading architects in the city he was appointed professor at the Nuremberg School of Building and he was a natural choice to found the Nuremberg branch of the German Architects Association (B.D.A.). He also dabbled in interior design and furniture design.

Ruff influenced the design of a number of buildings across Nuremberg and he was known for refusing to compromise his work. One building he was commissioned to design was a new Nuremberg City Hall on the banks of the Dutzendteich Lake and although arguments with the city council and the 1929 financial crisis scuppered the plans, they would come in useful later on.

Ruff's neo-baroque style of architecture was the Nazis' popular choice and when they seized power he became known to Gauleiter Julius Streicher. After Streicher introduced Ruff to Hitler, he was given his greatest commission, a new Congress Hall for the Rally Grounds. The chosen position was where the city council had wanted their new City Hall. Only this time there was no shortage of money and no red tape.

Ruff redrafted his City Hall plans and his son Franz presented them to the Führer in June 1934. The plans and the budget were immediately approved. With everything in place Ludwig Ruff was about to embark on his largest project when he was taken into a Nuremberg hospital for an operation. On 15 August 1934 he died unexpectedly. Franz Ruff continued his father's work.

Franz Ruff (1906–1979)

Ruff Junior followed in his father's footsteps and after training at the Nuremberg School of Building he studied architecture at Stuttgart and Berlin Technical Colleges. He was one of the many young men who found it impossible to find work after the German economy collapsed in 1929. Franz Ruff joined the NSDAP in 1931 and worked for the Nazis' favourite architect, Paul Ludwig Troost, as he converted the Gauleiter's offices on Marienplatz for Julius Streicher; the building would be known as known as the Hitlerhaus.

In 1932 Franz joined his father's Nuremberg office and later worked with him on the design for the new Congress Hall. Ludwig died just after Hitler commissioned the building and, despite his inexperience, 28-year-old Franz took over the project. His ability to please both Hitler and Streicher meant that he was showered with accolades and he succeeded his father as professor at the Nuremberg Academy of Art.

All of Franz Ruff's work came from the NSDAP, starting with the redesign of Cramer-Klett Villa, Gauleiter Streicher's new residence. He designed the extension to the Deutscher Hof Hotel, where Hitler stayed during the rallies, adding the balcony where Hitler stood as supporters marched past. He also converted the adjacent Siemens-Schtickert administrative building for the Führer's staff. Another Ruff project was the new Gauhaus next to the Hitlerhaus.

Work on the Congress Hall foundations was delayed by a high water table and they took two years to complete. Design changes by Hitler and disagreements between the design teams also hindered progress and by the time work was halted in 1940, engineers had still not worked out how to build the roof of the huge auditorium.

Ruff's design for the Congress Hall interior.

Franz Ruff's best known work was the SS barracks on Franconia road. His design was a simple imposing block with few architectural features, which could either be a result of his inexperience or his desire to create a functional building for an exacting master. Whatever the reason, the city council objected strongly, particularly to the need to purchase and demolish several buildings and move a tram line to make way for the barracks.

The council accused Ruff of bullying tactics as he tried to push his plans through and Heinrich Himmler finally intervened in the arguments, overruling the council. Work began in 1937 and for the next two years hundreds of labourers worked around the clock to finish the building.

The end of Nazi Germany in May 1945 ended Franz Ruff's lucrative career and he was classified as a Nazi follower by the Allies during the Denazification process. Even so, he was soon awarded a new project, a grandstand in Zerzabelshof, east of Nuremberg. He continued to work on minor architectural projects for the rest of his working life.

Albert Speer (1905–1981)

Speer was born in Mannheim but in 1918 his family moved to Heidelberg. He followed his father into architecture and studied at Karlsruhe University until he had raised the money to transfer to Munich Technical University. He transferred to Berlin Technical University in 1925 where he studied under renowned architect Heinrich Tessenow, becoming his assistant while he completed his postgraduate work.

Speer first heard Hitler speak at a Berlin rally in December 1930 and joined the NSDAP in March 1931. One of his first commissions was to redecorate the villa of Karl Hanke, the leader of west Berlin's NSDAP. Pay cuts at the university then forced him to return to Mannheim to work for his father.

While visiting Berlin in July 1932 Speer was introduced to Dr Joseph Goebbels by Hanke and he agreed to help renovate the NSDAP's new Berlin headquarters. Although Speer returned to Mannheim when the work was complete, Hanke invited him back to the capital when the Nazis took control the following year.

Goebbels was the new Propaganda Minister and he commissioned Speer to renovate the Ministry building. Hanke was now Goebbel's State Secretary and when Speer commented that his plans for the Berlin May Day commemoration would result in something resembling a rifle club meeting, he was challenged to come up with something better; he accepted. Speer used huge swastika flags as a backdrop and they proved to be the perfect focal point for the rally. Hitler was so impressed he asked Speer to work on designs for the 1933 Nuremberg Rally. Yet again the plans made an impact on the Führer and Speer was appointed 'Commissioner for the Artistic and Technical Presentation of Party Rallies and Demonstrations'.

Speer's next job was to liaise with the builders renovating the Berlin Chancellery to Paul Troost's design. Hitler was a challenging client and Speer's regular briefings brought him into the Führer's inner circle. The two men became close friends as they spent time discussing architecture and urban planning. Hitler had finally found someone who could turn his apparently limitless ideas into drawings and models.

Albert Speer with one of his designs.

When Paul Troost died on 21 March 1934, Speer was appointed the Party's Chief Architect and head of the Chief Office for Construction. One of his first tasks was to draw up an overall layout for the Nuremberg Rally Grounds and while his initial plan only covered the immediate area around the Luitpold Arena, he produced a grander plan in December 1934, including the Great Road, the Mars Field, the German Stadium and the Langwasser campsite. Although work on the campsite started immediately, it took time to design the new structures and work on the majority was abandoned when Germany went to war.

Speer invented the concept of 'ruin value', the design of large buildings that would turn into eye-catching ruins, lasting thousands of years. He was impressed by how Greek and Roman ruins symbolised the importance of their civilisations and he intended to do the same for the Third Reich with his own designs. Hitler warmed to the idea and he soon wanted to apply it to all new state buildings. It is impossible to consider this odd concept of immortality without thinking of Shelley's poem *Ozymandias* and its judgment on the powerful and their eventual, inevitable fate:

Hitler is given a guided tour of Luitpold Arena by Speer, Liebel and Streicher.

The final touches are made to the Zeppelin Field grandstand.

I met a traveller from an antique land
Who said: Two vast and trunkless legs of stone
Stand in the desert. Near them, on the sand,
Half sunk, a shattered visage lies…

… And on the pedestal these words appear:
'My name is Ozymandias, king of kings:
Look on my works, ye Mighty, and despair!'
Nothing beside remains. Round the decay
Of that colossal wreck, boundless and bare
The lone and level sands stretch far away.

The parallels with Hitler, the Third Reich and the Rally Grounds are too obvious to need pointing out.

Speer's reputation went from strength to strength as he pandered to Hitler's architectural pretensions, turning his fantastic ideas into plans and models. Although Werner March had been commissioned to design the Olympic Stadium for the 1936 Summer Olympics in Berlin, Hitler did not like the modern design. Speer was called in give the stadium a classical appearance and his redesign included a new stone exterior. He went on to design the German Pavilion for the 1937 International Paris exposition where it was awarded a gold medal.

Speer was appointed General Building Inspector for the Reich Capital, which gave him a huge influence over the Berlin City Council. During any consultation Speer would make it clear that he was answerable to Hitler alone.

In January 1938, Hitler commissioned Speer to start a huge new project in Berlin; a new Reich Chancellery on the same site as the original building. However, there were two problems. The site could not be cleared until April and it had to be ready for the next annual reception of foreign diplomats. Although Speer only had nine months to build the huge new structure, he did everything in his power to fulfil the Führer's wishes. Thousands of labourers worked around the clock in two shifts and the building was handed over, completely furnished, two days before the reception.

Hitler had grand designs for Berlin and Speer had to turn the Führer's implausible wish lists into working drawings and architectural models. The plans involved a complete rebuild of large parts of the city and the main feature would be a three-mile-long boulevard called the Street of Magnificence or the North-South Axis. The buildings were also on a large scale, rivalling those on the Rally Grounds. An assembly hall, with a domed roof over 210 metres high and capable of seating 180,000 people would stand at the north end, while a 120-metre-high triumphal arch would stand at the south end (the Paris Arc de Triomphe would fit inside the Berlin arch). The outbreak of war of course turned Hitler's attentions away from architecture and although Speer continued to work on his designs, building work was postponed and eventually abandoned.

THE DESIGNERS

While the three architects, Speer, Ruff senior and Ruff junior, designed the alterations to existing structures and drew up plans for new ones, they were supported by sculptors, craftsmen and stage designers.

Josef Thorak (1889–1952)

Thorak was born in Salzburg, Austria, and he learned about ceramics and pottery from his father. After qualifying in Vienna he continued his studies in Berlin in 1915, graduating in 1918. To begin with, Thorak worked with wax to attract commissions because he could not afford to cast in bronze. His first major work was a statue called The Dying Warrior (*Der Sterbende Krieger*), a sculpture for Stolpmünde's Great War memorial (Stolpmünde was in German Pomerania between the wars and is now called Ustka and in northwest Poland). After the Nazis seized power in 1933, Thorak was appointed one of the Third Reich's official sculptors.

Thorak was given a large government-funded studio near Munich and began work on numerous Nazi commissioned sculptures. His works were usually huge statues, up to 20 metres high, and they were often nude heroic figures or represented German folk-life. Thorak provided several sculptures for the 1936 Berlin Olympics stadium and he sculpted 'Comradeship', two enormous nude males, clasping hands in defiant poses for the German pavilion at the 1937 Paris World's Fair. His numerous studies of the human anatomy meant that he was sometimes called Professor Thorax.

The Rally Ground structures were built from rough brickwork hidden behind thin granite slabs.

The Nazis favoured huge sculptures of the male form.

Thorak's sculptures on the Nuremberg Rally Grounds included three female figures behind the Hall of Honour on the Luitpold Arena. The theme was the 'Victory of Work', with the figures representing physical and spiritual work. In 1937 Speer also commissioned him to create several heroic style pieces for the Mars Field. A group of huge bronze figures gathered around the goddess of victory was sculpted for the arena while two figures of horsemen would flank the entrance. Although Thorak spent many hours working on the sculptures, they were never displayed.

Thorak produced his final pieces for the House of German Art exhibition in 1944. Following the end of the war he lived in seclusion, a broken man. His large sculptures did not survive the war, but many smaller pieces did and in 1951 a collection was exhibited in the House of German Art. To Thorak's dismay, the exhibition caused a public outcry. He died the following year.

Arno Breker (1900–1991)

After studying architecture, sculpture and anatomy, the Westphalian Breker entered the Düsseldorf Academy of Arts to concentrate on sculpture. He initially concentrated on bronze busts but in 1927 he moved to Paris to extend his contacts in the art world. After travelling to North Africa he produced a series of lithographs titled the 'Tunisian Journey' and they were awarded a prize by the Prussian Ministry of Culture. After working in Rome he returned to Germany in 1934.

Following an introduction to Hitler, Breker joined the NSDAP and was appointed official State sculptor. He was soon appointed Professor of the Visual Arts in Berlin and was given a large property and studio.

Breker continued with his bust and portrait style sculptures until his work came to Albert Speer's attention and he was commissioned to sculpt two statues representing athletic prowess for the 1936 Berlin Olympic Games. Two of his sculptures were chosen by Albert Speer to stand at the entrance to the new Reich Chancellery and he commissioned him to produce other work for the Rally Grounds.

Most of Breker's work was destroyed by the Allies after the war and in 1948 he was fined for working on behalf of the Nazi regime. He returned to Düsseldorf and continued work as a sculptor.

Hermann Kaspar (1904–1986)

While Kaspar studied painting under Edmund Steppes and Carl Becker-Gundahl at the Academy of Fine Arts in Munich, it was his friendship with Speer that led to him becoming a Nazi favourite.

One of the eagles at the end of Luitpold Arena's Tribune of Honour.

After winning first prize for a mosaic frieze in Munich's German Museum in 1935, orders followed thick and fast. Hitler and Speer favoured his mosaics, especially his swastika pattern, and he was commissioned to tile the rooms of the Zeppelin Field grandstand. He went on to work on the interior design of the new Reich Chancellery in Berlin.

THE CITY PLANNERS

While the work of the architects such as Speer and Ruff is connected with the Nazis, the work of the urban planners is largely forgotten. The staff of Nuremberg City Council had to work with the Reich Party Rally Grounds Board, a board of officials appointed to make sure that the professionals carried out what the Nazis wanted. After the summer of 1934 they also had to work with 'Bureau Speer', a Berlin-based office with direct access to Hitler.

While the work on the main structures continued apace, the council and the Board had to make sure that a range of infrastructure projects, involving civil engineering, building construction, urban planning and landscaping, went ahead at the same fast pace. Thousands of unemployed people were put to work on the roads, paths, lawns and gardens that com-

The city council worked closely with the organisers to make the rallies run smoothly.

pleted the Rally Grounds. Everyone was ultimately working to please Hitler and Speer, and close cooperation was needed to meet schedules and overcome problems. Delays caused by red tape and differences in opinion would not be tolerated.

Walter Brugmann (1887–1944) had been head of the City Council Building Department since 1928 and in 1933 he was also appointed head of all urban development relating to the Rally Grounds. Wilhelm Schlegtendal and Heinz Schmeissner joined the building department around 1936 and they were both involved in the extensive urban planning; Schlegtendal was also involved with decorating Nuremberg's streets in the weeks leading up to the Reich Party Congress.

Alfred Hensel had been director of the City Council Gardens Department since 1922 and he designed the award-winning grounds that opened around the Municipal Stadium in 1928. He was appointed head of landscaping for the Luitpold Arena, the Congress Hall and the Zeppelin Field when Speer became involved in the Rally Grounds. Hensel had to make sure that the trees, hedges, flower beds and parks complemented the structures. When Speer's December 1934 plan increased the Rally Grounds to include the Great Road, the German Stadium and the Mars Field, Hensel was replaced by Gerhard Hinz.

Julius Schulte-Frohlinde had been a surveyor working for the urban planning department when he was asked to design the grandstand for Luitpold Arena in 1933. He was appointed head of the Beauty of Work Organisation (*Schönheit der Arbeit*), part of the German Labour Front, on Speer's recommendation in 1934. He set up his own building department and oversaw the development of many administration and training facilities. The Strength through Joy Village was one of his projects. (The seaside complex at Prora, on the Baltic Coast was another; it would become the largest construction project of the Nazi era).

6

THE INFRASTRUCTURE

The number of visitors to the rallies increased every year, rising from around 80,000 in 1923 to over 200,000 by the time the Nazis were in power in 1933. A staggering one million people visited Nuremberg's final rally in 1938. They all had to travel to and from the city, putting the rail network under tremendous pressure. Then also had to be accommodated and facilities ranged from top class venues for the senior party officials down to warehouses, schools and tents for the rank and file. Everyone had to be fed and watered as well.

The Nazis were anxious to make sure that everything passed off with military precision. The rallies were the time of year when the leadership were exposed to the people and the organisation of the rally reflected on the Party. What follows is a look at the massive efforts made to see that everyone went away with good memories; memories they would pass onto family and friends.

ACCOMMODATION DURING THE RALLIES

Hitler arrived at Nuremberg by rail and an SS guard was waiting to greet him at the station while a large fleet of cars were on hand to take him and his entourage to his accommodation. The NSDAP acquired a suite of rooms for Hitler's use during his political campaigning in the city. They were in the Deutscher Hof Hotel, next to the Nuremberg Opera House on Frauentorgraben, a road running parallel to the city's medieval wall.

When the Nazis came to power, Hitler's entourage increased dramatically and the adjacent Siemens administration building was acquired to accommodate them all. It was converted under Franz Ruff's direction and the rooms and offices were ready in time for the 1936 rally. The main change to the exterior of the hotel was a balcony overlooking the main road, where Hitler could watch the parades from; it also gave the crowds a better view of their Führer.

Senior Party leaders were booked into the city's best hotels to begin with but the Nazis took steps to buy entire buildings once they were in power. By 1936 the NSDAP had acquired several buildings for their exclusive use. The Grand Hotel in Bahnhofplatz,

Hitler salutes a march past from the new balcony of the Deutscher Hof Hotel.

SA units march back into the Langwasser camp after a long day in the city.

next to the railway station, was demolished following the 1936 rally and a new NSDAP guesthouse with 142 rooms was ready in only seven months. It was never occupied for more than three weeks a year. A new hotel with a similar number of beds was built on Weidenkellerstraße, around the corner from the Führer's hotel, but it was not ready until 1939. The National Socialist press corps stayed in Frankischer Hof Hotel in Eilgutstraße, close to the railway station. The hotel was a modernised building with 161 rooms.

While the Party leaders stayed in the top hotels, the rank and file stayed in a range of schools, factories and public buildings across the city. A late fifteenth-century five-storey stable in the grounds of Nuremberg Castle was just one of many buildings requisitioned by the Nazis. The Imperial Stables (*Kaiserstallung*) were converted into a youth hostel for 450 boys and it opened in time for the 1938 rally. This was, however, a drop in the ocean as far as accommodation was concerned.

While the senior NSDAP members, government officials and high-ranking military officers enjoyed luxury hotel accomodation, the tens of thousands of members of the rank and file stayed on a military-style campsite in the Langwasser area south of Dutzendteich Lakes.

The area belonged to the Bavarian State Forestry Administration and while part of it had been used as a firing range during the First World War, it was abandoned after the Armistice. The area came under scrutiny when Nuremberg City Council discussed plans for a new suburb in 1926 and part of the wooded area was cleared to make way for a new urban development.

By 1932 Nuremberg City Housing Corporation was planning a second development and the Bavarian State Forestry Administration handed over 600 acres to the council. However, the plans never got off the drawing board because Speer's December 1934 plan for the Rally Grounds included new camping grounds in the Langwasser area.

The area was confiscated from Nuremberg City Council early in 1935 and the Reich Labour Service started work on turning the area into a huge campsite. The plan was for each of the party organisations, including the SS, the SA, the Reich Labour Service and the Hitler Youth, to have their own areas, each one laid out like a military camp.

Over the next four years Speer's plans were realised as Langwasser campsite expanded to 950 hectares (2350 acres), enough space for several hundred thousand people to live for the week. Men of the Reich Labour Service worked all year round on the camp, installing roads, hard standings, water pipes, sewers and electricity cables. Activity increased in the weeks before the rally to make the campsite ready. As the day loomed the men began erecting dozens of enormous tents ready for the visitors.

The largest camp grounds belonged to the SA and the final extension was completed in 1937, creating a rectangular area of approximately 1000 x 850 metres. While the number of tents increased to accommodate the extra number of visitors each year, the shape and layout of the camp remained roughly the same. In 1937 the camp was divided into four equal quadrants and each one had 99 large white tents set out in three straight double

An aerial view of the huge camp site.

Mobile kitchens dished up tens of thousands of meals a day.

rows. Each tent measured 35 x 12 metres and had enough room for 250 men; a *Sturmbann* or battalion occupied four tents. The whole area could accommodate nearly 100,000 SA men. Each man brought his own bed roll and found a place on the straw scattered on the ground inside the tent.

The four quadrants were separated by two intersecting streets and they met in the centre at a round space named Horst-Wessel-Platz. Staff at the horseshoe-shaped command post answered queries from unit commanders and dealt with problems caused by the rank and file. Guards manning the wooden watchtower kept an eye on the camp. Camping style ablution blocks were erected at regular intervals while twelve large wooden supply blocks were built along two sides of the square.

Similar camps were planned for the SS, the Hitler Youth and other party organisations to the east of the SA camp but they were never completed. After 1937 the Hitler Youth stayed on an area previously used for storage while other groups were allocated camping spaces around the city, either in factories or on parkland or waste ground. Neither the Reich Labour Service camp in the Moorenbrunn area nor the National Socialist Motor Corps camp between Gliwice Road and Oelser Road were built. A camp was planned for junior Party officials but only the roads had been built by 1938 and they continued to be housed in factories, school buildings and restaurants.

The thousands of visitors on the Langwasser camp required a huge amount of water for drinking and washing. Speer had a water tower built on a hill called Hohen Bühl, east of the camp. The masonry tower was covered with stonework and ready for use in time for the 1938 Rally.

Labourers worked around the clock to get everything ready for the annual rally.

The thousands of labourers needed something more permanent to live in while they worked on the Rally Grounds. They also had to live close to the worksite. An abandoned factory on the Regensburg road was converted into a large workers camp while two nearby blocks were converted into a mixture of four- and six-bed dormitories. The dining hall and kitchen fed around 1200 workers every day. A smaller camp was set up for labourers working on the SS barracks.

The Nazis also went to extraordinary lengths to make Nuremberg the perfect city. A large number of invalid war veterans lived in the city and the majority were unemployed and homeless. The Nazis did not want to see them begging on the streets during the Reich Party Congress and they acquired a piece of land on the Regensburg road in 1933 to house them. The German Labour Front started work on a four-storey complex but by 1938 only half of the 336 apartments were complete.

Altenfurt e.V. (*eingetragener Verein*) Association (Altenfurt is a suburb of Nuremberg) started work on another apartment complex and Deputy Gauleiter Karl Holz named it after Julius Streicher when the roof of the first block was completed in May 1934. Although the block was used as a school, the children had to move out each year to make way for the army of volunteer workers arriving to work on the Rally Grounds. The German Workers Front had to take over the development when the Altenfurt e.V. Association ran out of money in 1937.

TRANSPORT TO AND FROM THE RALLIES

While the amount of time and money lavished on the Rally Grounds is obvious, the Nazis had to spend a similar amount of effort on the transport system. The nature of the rally was such that everyone wanted to arrive around the same time and then leave around the same time to limit the amount of time taken off work. The tens of thousands of visitors had to get in and out without a hitch, otherwise they would leave with a bad impression of the rallies and of the Nazi Party. If the Party could not organise a rally, how could they organise the country? There was a lot to plan, design, finance and build while each new feature had to be completed before the next rally. Road and rail facilities around Nuremberg were continuously improved and extended and yet again money was no object.

The Railway Network
Most of the visitors to the Nuremberg Rallies travelled by train and the rallies were a testing time for the German Reich Railways. In 1933 only one double railway line passed the east side of the Rally Grounds and everyone came and went via Dutzendteich station. By 1938 new lines had been laid and new stations had been added.

Cars wait at Nuremberg station to take senior Party officials to their accommodation.

Dutzendteich station was a small structure to the east of the Zeppelin Field and it was too small. Speer ordered its demolition when he became involved in the Rally Grounds in April 1934 and its replacement was completed by August, in time for the September rally.

Reich Railways architect Fritz Limpert based the design on a station in Berlin's suburbs, where the crowds headed every summer. While it only had a small station building, the platforms were increased to 200 metres in length, allowing longer trains to use it. Passengers were shepherded through the 18 booths and then formed up into their units ready to start the long march to Langwasser camp.

In September 1934 the first specially chartered trains arrived during the early hours of the morning and the trains pulled away as soon as the men stepped onto the platform. The officers barked out orders to form up and the SA units began the long walk to their billets. Trains pulled into Dutzendteich station every few minutes and continued to do so until the 122nd pulled out late in the afternoon. There would be far more in the years to come.

A Berlin SA unit arrives in Nuremberg after a long journey.

A second pair of tracks and a new station were added in 1936 while underpasses allowed passengers to walk beneath the railway. It was still not enough for the growing number of visitors and Speer planned a new four-track branch line running between the March Field and Langwasser Camp.

Work started on the huge Mars Field station in 1937; the long station had 64 exit doors and underpasses at each end so that passengers could get off the platform as quickly as possible; they then faced only a short march to their campsite. It was only half ready by September 1938 and by the time work had been completed it was too late; the 1939 rally was cancelled.

Another station was planned for the south side of the Langwasser campsite to serve the camps for the SS and Party officials. Although work started on Fischbach station in 1937, it took until 1940 to complete.

The number of visitors to Nuremberg kept increasing and by 1938 specially chartered trains carried around 700,000 spectators and 560,000 participants to the Rally Grounds efficiently and without delays. It was a remarkable feat for the German Reich Railways.

The Autobahn Network

Hitler's commitment to Germany's autobahn network was made on 1 May 1933 and the first stretch was opened between Frankfurt and Darmstadt in May 1935. Construction continued at a rapid pace but while over 500 miles of autobahn were opened for traffic

Hitler opens a new section of autobahn.

each year, very few people could afford a car to drive on it. For example, while the number of motor vehicles in Nuremberg was only 30,000 in 1938, the annual number of passenger journeys around the city rose from 3.5 million to 6.3 million; there were 1.25 million visitors to the rally ground alone. Drivers also faced a city-wide ban on motor vehicles during rally week. Everyone either had to walk or use a bicycle.

Long-distance motor bus routes were also a new phenomenon and the first routes from Berlin and Munich did not start until 1938. Both routes had been laid on especially for the rallies and they only stopped at Nuremberg station and the Rally Grounds.

Even so, the Nazis spent 3.5 million Reich Marks on motorways and slip roads around the Rally Grounds between 1933 and 1940. In September 1937 the motorway linking Bayreuth and Nuremberg opened, providing a direct link to Berlin. It ran south east of the Rally Grounds and slip roads connected with Münchener Straße to the west and Regensburger Straße to the east; another slip road was added to the west in February 1938.

The autobahn link to Munich was opened, in spite of many construction problems, by Gauleiter Streicher and Inspector General Fritz Todt just before the September 1938 rally. A three-mile stretch of the Nuremberg to Stuttgart motorway opened at the same time to the south side of the Rally Grounds.

ACHIEVING THE LOOK

Albert Speer's designs were made to look as if they were made from solid white granite, like the temples of antiquity. While they did look impressive when they were finished, he cheated to keep costs and building time down. The structures were built of rough brickwork and clad with thin granite slabs. The Nazis also went to extreme lengths to procure the perfect materials at the lowest price.

The *Art of the Third Reich* magazine championed the advantage of using granite in new Reich buildings in the one of its articles:

> Never before has such a wealth of precious natural stones been pulled out from German soil for new buildings. The finest rocks come from all German regions and German business people from all regions have had the chance to share in this great and unique creation. This monument to German will and energy is taken from the German soil, mastered and shaped by German artisans and built to the Führer's ideas and instructions under the direction of Albert Speer.

While the article made it sound as if Germans were putting their heart and soul into producing the new buildings of the Third Reich, this was of course a lie. The SS used its contacts to undercut legitimate businesses while slave labourers rather than masons quarried the granite.

During the first five years of the Third Reich the demand for granite was small and companies were able to supply government contracts from existing quarries. However, by 1938 the quantity needed for the Rally Grounds in Nuremberg and other buildings in cities

Mayor Liebel, Hitler, Speer and Martin Bormann meet the workforce.

across Germany, particularly Berlin, was far greater than what they could supply. Although the quarry owners formed cooperatives to provide large amounts of granite quickly, it was going to be expensive. There was also a new competitor – and that was the SS.

By 1938 the Main SS Economic and Administrative Department (the *SS-Wirtschafts und Verwaltungshauptamt* or WVHA) was managing business projects on behalf of the General SS (Allegemeine-SS) and it controlled the organisation's finances. It also ran the concentration camp system and the thousands of prisoners were free labour. Office Group W (*Amtsgruppe W*) controlled the production, manufacture and distribution of several building products and they were either sold directly through government contracts or through bogus companies. SS Obergruppenführer Oswald Pohl and his deputy SS Gruppenführer Georg Lörner had been busy looking for new ways to fill the SS coffers and they planned to use their contacts to make money from lucrative government contracts.

Pohl came from Duisburg and joined the navy after leaving school, serving with it throughout the First World War. He began studying law after the war but dropped out to become a paymaster for a Berlin Freikorps paramilitary unit. Although he rejoined the navy in 1924 he soon enrolled in the SA and the NSDAP. He met Heinrich Himmler in 1933 and was appointed chief of his administration department. In June 1935 he was promoted to administration chief and Reich treasurer for the SS and then established the Concentration Camp Inspectorate (*Inspektion der Konzentrationslager*) to run the expanding concentration camp system.

In April 1938, Pohl and Lörner set up the German Earth and Stone Works (*Deutsche Erd und Steinwerke GmbH* or DEST), a commercial operation to produce bricks and quarry granite. Its headquarters were located in Sankt Georgen an der Gusen, a small Austrian town near Linz (it was close to where Mauthausen concentration camp opened in August 1938). Their own headquarters were set up at Flossenbürg, in the northern Upper Palatinate.

They used political contacts to obtain supply contracts and to find the sites for quarries and brickworks, pricing in their endless supply of slave labour to undercut their rivals. They then established their first concentration camp at Flossenbürg in May 1938 and moved prisoners into it to begin quarrying granite.

In June 1939 Pohl became combined head of the SS Administration and Economy Office (*Hauptamt Verwaltung und Wirtschaft*) and the Budget and Construction Office (*Hauptamt Haushalt und Bauten*). The two offices eventually combined into the SS Economic and Administrative Department (*SS-Wirtschafts-Verwaltungshauptamt* or WVHA) in February 1942. (Oswald Pohl was sentenced to death for war crimes in Nuremberg in 1947; he was executed in 1951.)

The first prisoners arrived in Flossenbürg in May 1938 and they set about building the first concentration camp set up specifically for granite quarrying. Mauthausen concentration camp was set up near Linz in August 1938; Gusen camp would open nearby in April 1940. Groß-Rosen satellite camp opened near Sachsenhausen concentration camp, Lower Silesia, in August 1940 and it became an independent camp the following spring.

Concentration camp labour quarries granite for the Nuremberg Rally Grounds.

Natzweiler–Struthof concentration camp opened southwest of Strasbourg in May 1941 to provide the red stone for the outside of the German Stadium. Most of the granite slabs were never used.

To begin with most of the inmates were German and Austrian men arrested for crimes and antisocial behaviour. Czechs were used after the occupation of Czechoslovakia and Poles following the invasion. Slave labour from the Soviet Union would be used after Operation Barbarossa in June 1941. However, few of the foreign prisoners would quarry granite because construction work on the Nuremberg Rally Grounds had virtually halted; instead they worked on defence industry contracts.

The prisoners were forced to do back-breaking work for long hours in the quarries. The inhuman conditions, poor diet and lack of safety measures meant that accidents, injuries and deaths were common place. They were forced to work in extreme temperatures in the winter with no gloves, no socks and sometimes no shoes, yet anyone who reported sick was given 25 lashes.

Albert Speer stated that he had no knowledge of the Holocaust when he was tried at Nuremberg and then again in his memoirs, but his designs benefited from the concentration camp system. He was appointed Minister of War in February 1942 and over the next three years his Ministry exploited slave labour across the Reich.

Speer returned to Nuremberg in October 1945 for the year-long trials. He was found guilty of war crimes and crimes against humanity and sentenced to 20 years imprisonment. He served them all.

7

THE PARTICIPANTS

Many different organisations attended the Nuremberg rallies and each one had its day of parades. The Reich Labour Service was the first to march in front of the Führer on the Zeppelin Field. The Hitler Youth assembled in the Franken Stadium while the SS and the SA gathered in the Luitpold Arena. The armed forces closed the rally with military manoeuvres on the Zeppelin Field.

What follows are short histories of each organisation and short biographies of their leaders who spoke to the Party faithful at the rallies.

THE ARMED FORCES

Following the end of the First World War Germany's armed forces were severely restricted under the Treaty of Versailles signed in June 1919. Articles 160 to 210 limited the Reichswehr to 100,000 troops, banned conscription and placed restrictions on weapons and equipment. Paramilitary units, called Free Corps, were formed to get around the ban and they were involved in civil disturbances across the country. When the Nazis came to power in 1933, they looked to increase size of the armed forces and arm them with up-to-date weapons and equipment. Each year the military revue on the Zeppelin Field was one of the highlights of the Nuremberg Rally.

In May 1935 compulsory conscription was introduced, creating many new army units. Labour service was made obligatory in June 1935 and 200,000 men joined work battalions on labour-intensive schemes. The Nazis saw them as training units for the armed forces and it was a short step from carrying a shovel to shouldering a rifle. Conscription was increased to two years in August 1936 and by the time Germany invaded Poland in 1939, it had ¾ million men on active service and another million in reserve.

The Treaty of Versailles also banned Germany from possessing military aircraft but the commercial airline, Lufthansa, and gliding clubs, trained pilots and aircrew. In March 1933 Reich Air Commissioner Herman Göring was appointed head of the Reich Air Travel Ministry; it was only a cover for a new military air force. In March 1935, Göring

Motorised artillery units drive past the incomplete Zeppelin Tribune.

announced he was Commander-in-Chief of the Luftwaffe and it had 1900 planes and over 20,000 officers and men; the numbers shocked the world. It would have 4000 military planes by the summer of 1939.

THE ARMED FORCE COMMANDERS

General Werner von Blomberg was appointed Minister of Defence on 1 January 1933 and he played an important part in helping the Nazis to secure control over the armed forces. He called upon officers to make an oath of loyalty to the Führer following President Paul von Hindenburg's death in August 1934 and was appointed head of the new Wehrmacht in May 1935 while Hitler became Supreme Commander. After Blomberg objected to Hitler's plans for war, he was forced to resign in January 1938 following a fabricated scandal involving his new wife. The post of the Minister of Defence was abolished and Wilhelm Keitel (1882–1946) was appointed to the new post as Chief of the High Command of the Armed Forces.

The three armed services had their own commanders, each with their own staff. Commander-in-Chief of the Army, Generaloberst Kurt von Hammerstein Equord (1878–1943), lobbied against the appointment of Hitler as Chancellor in January 1933 and was forced to resign in January 1934. Generaloberst Werner von Fritsch (1880–1939)

Admiral Raeder, General Blomberg and General Fritsch enjoy the manoeuvres.

went on to supervise the rapid expansion and rearmament of the army until he protested against Hitler's plan to wage war in November 1937. He was falsely accused of homosexual offences and forced to resign in February 1938. Generaloberst Walther von Brauchitsch (1881–1948) attended the last Nuremberg rally in September 1938.

Generalfeldmarshall Hermann Göring (1893–1946) represented the German Air Force and the Luftwaffe made its first appearance at the rallies in 1935. Although the German Navy could not take part in the rallies, their Chief of the Naval High Command, Generaladmiral Erich Raeder (1876–1960) attended.

THE PROTECTION ECHELON, THE SCHUTZSTAFFEL (SS)

The SS began life in 1925 as an eight-man bodyguard chosen by Julius Schreck to protect Hitler after he was released from Landsberg prison. By September, additional bodyguard details had been formed at each district NSDAP headquarters to protect local leaders. Erhard Heiden was appointed Reichsführer-SS in 1927 but membership declined and the 280-strong organisation was taken over by his deputy, Heinrich Himmler, in January 1929. Membership increased rapidly over the next four years and the organisation was divided into brigades and regiments.

The SS numbered nearly 50,000 when Hitler was made Chancellor in January 1933 and SS units acted as auxiliary police units, rounding up enemies of the State following the Reichstag fire in February. The Leibstandarte-SS Adolf Hitler was soon organised under Joseph Dietrich as the core of the Armed Troops-SS (*Verfügungstruppe-SS*) separating it from the General SS (the Allgemeine-SS), the business side of Himmler's empire.

A new concentration camp at Dachau, near Munich, became a model camp and the SS soon took control of all the concentration camps across Germany. At the end of June 1934 the Leibstandarte-SS Adolf Hitler rounded up opponents of the Nazi regime (and many leaders of the SA) during the Night of the Long Knives, executing many of their victims. A month later the SS was formally separated from the SA.

By 1939 the SS had grown into a huge organisation encompassing the State police, the Party police, armed units, a network of concentration camps and a large business empire employing camp labour. A large part of this slave labour was employed quarrying stone for the Nuremberg Rally Grounds.

SS units fill the centre of Luitpold Arena.

Himmler and Dietrich accompany Hitler during an inspection of the SS guard of honour.

Commander of the SS

Heinrich Himmler (1900–1945) gained an agriculture diploma at Munich Technical College before becoming a laboratory technician. He joined Ernst Röhm's Reich War Flag Freekorps unit but after carrying their flag during the 1923 Munich Putsch he returned to Landshut to run a chicken farm. He was appointed Party propaganda leader in 1925, deputy leader of the Schutzstaffel in 1926, and Reichsführer-SS in January 1929.

Himmler was also appointed chief of the Munich police after the Nazis seized power in January 1933 and the SS soon expanded its control of the German police. He was given control of the Gestapo and control of all police activities outside Prussia in April 1934. Himmler was finally handed control of all police activities across Germany in June 1936. The merging of State and Party police activities under Reinhard Heydrich's Reich Main Security Office in September 1939 completed Himmler's empire of political oppression.

THE STORM DIVISION (STURM ABTEILUNG OR SA)

The SA's beginnings were in protecting the German Worker's Party political meetings. The name was adopted in November 1921 after a fierce battle in the Hofbräuhaus in Munich and unit standards were presented at the first Party Rally in Munich in January 1923. Hermann Göring organised the SA into regiments, battalions and companies and while the Transport Division (*Vehrkehrsabteilung*) provided vehicles, the Field Jäger Corps (*Feldjägerkorps*) guarded political meetings and the Staff Guard (*Stabswache*) protected leaders. The SA was banned following the Munich Putsch in November 1923 but Ernst Röhm kept it going under the name *Frontbann*.

The SA reformed in February 1925 under Heinrich von Helldorf and then Franz Pfeffer von Salomon took command. He left after a disagreement in August 1930 and following a revolt in Berlin, Hitler took command until Ernst Röhm returned from Bolivia in January 1931. Röhm introduced military training and made sure the SA played an important role in bringing politics onto the streets, through violence. He also quadrupled membership to 400,000 in twelve months.

Hitler was appointed Chancellor in January 1933 and two months later the SA were turned into an auxiliary police force responsible for arresting political opponents and holding them in makeshift Wild Camps, the precursor to concentration camps. They then occupied trade union offices and arrested their leaders in May.

The SA often staged boycotts of Jewish businesses but their auxiliary police status was removed in August because they were getting out of hand. Although thousands of SA members proudly marched through Nuremberg a month later, the organisation was struggling to find a new role in the Third Reich.

Membership increased dramatically to 4.5 million when it absorbed the Steel Helmet ex-serviceman's organisation in 1934, making it nearly 50 times the size of Germany's standing army, the Reichswehr. Röhm's calls to merge the SA and the Reichswehr into a national militia, or People's Army, infuriated Nazi leaders and alarmed army generals. His

SA units parade through Adolf-Hitler-Platz in the centre of Nuremberg.

talk of a Second Revolution against the establishment threatened to undermine Hitler's position. He was even critical of Hitler and by the spring of 1934 the time had come to curb the organisation.

The Nazi leadership demanded action as rumours of an SA revolt increased and the SS fabricated information confirming Röhm's intentions. On 30 June Röhm and dozens of senior SA officers across the country were arrested and murdered by the SS in the Blood Purge, or Night of the Long Knives.

Viktor Lutze was appointed Chief of Staff but when the SA paraded in front of Hitler at Nuremberg, it was a shadow of its former self. The SS, however, was made an independent organisation and its members were given pride of place in the 1934 rally. Actions against unruly elements of the SA were stepped up and membership fell rapidly as young men were conscripted into the Labour Service and the armed forces; it was only 1.6 million strong by the time of the 1935 rally.

Storm Division Commanders

There were several commanders of the SA but it was Ernst Röhm (1887–1934) who turned it into the organisation seen on the Luitpold Arena at Nuremberg. Röhm served

Hitler and Ernst Röhm walk across Luitpold Arena.

as an officer in the German Army in the trenches and then with the Free Corps on the streets before serving as a Captain in the Reichswehr. He used his hidden cache of weapons to help bring down the Communist government in Munich in 1919. Röhm was impressed by Hitler and his followers took part in the Munich Putsch in November 1923. He was arrested but released on probation and emigrated to Bolivia to work as a military instructor.

Röhm returned to Germany to command the SA and membership increased dramatically under his leadership. By the spring of 1934 the SA had 4,500,000 members but the Führer's distrust of Röhm increased, partly because of rumours of a move against Hitler by the SA leader apparently initiated by the French and then based upon a dossier of manufactured evidence prepared by Heydrich and Himmler. On 30 June 1934, Hitler arrested the SA leader in Bad Wiessee, Bavaria, and two days later he was murdered. He was replaced by Viktor Lutze (1890–1943).

Lutze served in the trenches in the First World War and he joined the NSDAP and the SA in 1922. He became deputy Gauleiter for the Ruhr in 1925 and was voted into the Reichstag in September 1930. After the Nazis seized power he was appointed police president of Hannover and a member of the Prussian State Council; he was also promoted to SA-Obergruppenführer.

Lutze told Hitler about the plans to turn the SA into an army and then accompanied the Führer when he arrested Röhm. Lutze was appointed SA leader with orders to curb bad behaviour. The SA was quickly reduced to training duties under his command.

THE REICH LABOUR SERVICE (REICHSARBEITSDIENST OR RAD)

The Depression doubled Germany's unemployment from 2.9 million in 1929 to 6 million by 1933; 30 per cent of the workforce. Although the Weimar government placed 250,000 men with the Volunteer Labour Service, the Nazis intended to put far more to work on agricultural and construction projects.

While the Nazis boycotted the Volunteer Labour Service, they announced their first Law for the Reduction of Unemployment in June 1933. 1000 million Reichsmarks were budgeted for new Emergency Work Programmes and thousands of men were employed on farms, dams and autobahns. Another 500 million Reichsmarks were pledged when a second law was enacted in September and new environmental projects including forestry, land reclamation and river improvement projects were announced. Unemployed men were offered places in labour battalions, reducing unemployment and creating a cheap workforce for public works schemes. Existing volunteer organisations were merged into the National Socialist Volunteer Labour Service and it was renamed the Reich Labour Service in 1934.

A law of June 1935 introduced obligatory labour service for all unemployed males between the ages of 19 and 25 and 200,000 men at a time were summoned to work in camps for six months at a time. Skills and qualifications were ignored and they were counted as employed, even though they were unpaid.

Reich Labour Service units march past the Zeppelin Tribune.

Konstantin Hierl, head of the Reich Labour Service, stands to the left of Hitler.

The length of labour service was first increased to one year and then to two years in August 1936, helping to reduce unemployment to 1.6 million. By September 1939, there were 750,000 men working for the Reich Labour Service and another million in reserve; there were also 250,000 young women, or Labour Maids, employed in the service industry, allowing young men to be reemployed in the rearmament industries.

The Reich Labour Service gave rudimentary military training, preparing young men for the armed forces. At the Reich Labour Service rally labour battalions paraded on the Zeppelin Field shouldering shovels rather than rifles.

Head of the Reich Labour Service

In September 1919 Konstantin Hierl (1875–1955) was a major in the Reichswehr's political department in Munich when he ordered Hitler to observe the German Worker's Party. The order led to Hitler joining the Party and eventually becoming the leader of the NSDAP. Hierl also joined the NSDAP and was appointed head of the Volunteer Labour Service in 1931. He became head of the National Socialist Labour Service in 1933 and it was renamed the Reich Labour Service in 1934.

THE GERMAN LABOUR FRONT (DEUTSCHE ARBEITSFRONT OR DAF)

The Nazis viewed trade unions as relics of the Marxist class struggle and their offices were subjected to random attacks as soon as they seized power. While the unions wanted to work with the NSDAP they were going to be replaced by a State-run workers' organisation. On 1 May 1933, labour rallies were held across the country but the following day SA troopers and NSBO (National Socialist Factory Cell Organisation) representatives occupied union offices across Germany. Over the week that followed, around 150 trade unions were disbanded, their assets were seized and their leaders imprisoned.

On 10 May the German Labour Front, a State-controlled union organised from region down to shop floor, was announced. New Labour Offices were also opened, offering job opportunities for Party members. The Front then used the unions' money and property to assist workers, hold vocational courses and run a workers' recreational organisation called Strength through Joy (Kraft durch Freude).

Head of the German Labour Front

Dr Robert Ley (1890–1945) served as a pilot in the First World War and he joined the NSDAP in 1924 while working as a chemist. His crude and drunken behaviour made him unpopular with many Nazi leaders but his fierce anti-Semitism and loyalty to Hitler assured his success. He was elected to the Prussian *Landtag* in 1928 and the Reichstag in 1930. He became Party Organisation Leader in 1932. On 10 May 1933, Robert Ley was appointed head of the new German Labour Front at the head of 20 million workers.

Robert Ley stands at Hitler's
shoulder.

THE HITLER YOUTH

Hitler announced the founding of the Youth League in May 1922. Boys aged 16 to 18 joined Young Storm Troops and boys aged 14 to 16 were organised into Young Men's Groups; they both reported to the SA. 900 members attended the Remembrance Day parade in Nuremberg in September 1922 and a month later, Hitler presented the organisation with their first flag in Coburg. The Youth League was banned after the Munich Beer Hall Putsch in November 1923 but it reformed at the same time as the NSDAP, at the beginning of 1925.

Kurt Gruber soon replaced Edmund Heines as the Youth League commander and he separated it from the SA, reorganised it in the same way as the NSDAP and introduced a uniform. The name Hitler Youth, or Hitlerjugend, was used after the summer of 1925 and it was formally adopted at the Weimar Party Rally in July 1926. Boys aged 10 to 14 could join Young Folk, or Jungvolk, units after 1928.

Membership remained low until Baldur von Schirach became involved and he organised youth leaders into *Rings* and boys aged 15 to 18 into *Scharen* (which roughly translates as gatherings or rallies). Schirach saw to it that the Hitler Youth reported once more to the SA in April 1931 and took command in June 1932.

The Hitler Youth went from strength to strength over the next six years, offering military style activities, including roll calls, war games, parades, shooting, hiking and map reading to its members. Sporting activities encouraged competitiveness and improved physical fitness, while older boys worked on farms.

A busy schedule of activities during the weekly Home Evenings turned a boy's unit into his home from home and every boy had a Performance Booklet to record his progress. They often worked alongside the SA, promoting propaganda activities, parades and recruitment drives.

The Day of the State Youth was a huge summer athletic events but for many boys the Day of the Hitler Youth at the Nuremberg Rallies was the highlight of the year. By 1935 over 60 per cent of German boys were in the Hitler Youth and 54,000 boys heard Hitler tell them to be 'as swift as a greyhound, as tough as leather and as hard as Krupp steel' at the September Rally.

Membership for boys over 15 was obligatory after December 1936 and new organisations were formed to train them in military-style activities. The Hitler Youth Flier Corps prepared teenagers for the Luftwaffe, the Hitler Youth Marine Corps trained them for

Hitler Youth drummers await the Führer's entrance into the stadium.

the navy, the Hitler Youth Equestrian Corps had links with cavalry units, the Hitler Youth Motor Corps trained mechanics, the Hitler Youth Communications Corps covered signalling and there was a musical section. A separate organisation trained youths for the SS.

Over 80,000 members converged on Nuremberg in September 1936 to hear the Führer's instructions:

> You, my youth, are our nation's most precious guarantee for a great future, and you are destined to be the leaders of a glorious new order under the supremacy of National Socialism. Never forget that one day you will rule the world!

In March 1939 it was a legal requirement for children to join one of the Reich youth organisations and the State could place children in orphanages if their parents objected.

Hitler Youth units were organised like army units, with departments covering leadership, propaganda, labour service, hygiene, sanitation, youths abroad and aviation training. The boys wore military-style uniforms and while their black armband had a single runic S, each unit had a triangular patch; specialist units had their own insignia. It was not difficult to see that Germany's youth was being prepared for war.

The German Girls League

The NSDAP formed a small female youth group as early as 1923 and the Hitler Youth Sisterhood was organised in 1928 for girls over 14; it was renamed the German Girls League (*Bund Deutscher Mädel*) in July 1930. Young Girls Groups were organised in April 1931 for girls over the age of ten.

The girls took part in the same activities as boys to begin with, but female-orientated activities, encouraging comradeship, physical fitness and the practice of feminine crafts were introduced later. The girls gathered regularly to play music, sing songs and engage in arts and crafts.

The League uniform included a long navy blue skirt, a white blouse and a brown jacket while hair was worn in twin pigtails. Membership of the German Girls League was made compulsory in 1936 for girls over 15 and before long there were two million members.

The Faith and Beauty (*Glaube und Schönheit*) organisation was established in 1937 to teach young ladies aged 17 to 21 how to be good National Socialist wives and mothers. They trained for marriage and motherhood, taking courses in household activities, domestic science and fashion design; physical education and sporting events also played an important part in the curriculum.

The German Girls League was generally excluded from the Nuremberg Rally but it held its first rally in 1936 in Bamberg, 40 miles north of Nuremberg. The girls paraded in a stadium to listen to speeches by their leaders and participated in a sports festival. They then gathered in front of Bamberg Cathedral to make a night-time pledge to the Führer.

A delegation of 5000 girls was invited to the Hitler Youth Day and trains shuttled them from Bamberg to Nuremberg. No doubt the rest felt they had missed out after hearing stories from Nuremberg.

A train chartered by the German Girls League arrives in Nuremberg.

Head of the Hitler Youth

There were several Hitler Youth leaders during the early days of the organisation but it was Baldur von Schirach (1907–1974) who turned it into the organisation which attended the Nuremberg Rallies. Schirach joined the NSDAP and the Munich SA in 1925 and came into contact with many leading Nazis after marrying Henny Hoffmann, the daughter of the Party photographer, Heinrich Hoffmann. He was often scorned for his effeminate behaviour but a stream of complimentary poetry about Hitler kept him in the Führer's close circle.

Schirach joined the National Socialist Students' League and the National Socialist Pupils' League in 1928, and became leader of the Students' League the following year. The League actively targeted student issues and it was soon more popular than fraternities in many universities. Schirach's organisational skills did not go unnoticed and he was appointed the Hitler Youth Leader in October 1931. He became Reich Youth Leader in June 1933 and spoke at all the rallies held in the Franken Stadium. As the rumours about his effeminate behaviour increased, Schirach joined the Wehrmacht in December 1939.

Hess, Hitler and Baldur von Schirach in front of the Hitler Youth.

REICH WOMEN'S LEAGUE (REICH FRAUENSHAFT)

Women's emancipation introduced millions of new voters to the world of German politics and over 11 million women were working after the First World War, many of them in traditional male occupations. However, Hitler opposed feminism and women's liberation and the NSDAP programme defined the woman's role as supporting her husband and raising her children. Slogans such as *Kinder, Küche, Kirche,* 'Children, Church, Kitchen', 'the women's place is in the home' and 'the wooden spoon is as important a weapon as a rifle' summarised the Nazis' view of women's role in society. But while the Party excluded women from direct involvement in politics, it worked hard to secure their votes.

Once in power the Nazis implemented policies limiting women's options, encouraging them to marry and raise families rather than work or go to university. Women were discriminated against by employers and by 1937, 800,000 had been pressured into marrying, reducing male unemployment. They were also encouraged to have children, and while

Gertrud Scholtz-Klink speaks
in the Luitpold Hall.

large families received financial incentives, childless couples were taxed at a higher rate and
denounced as 'worse than deserters on the battlefield'.

Isbeth Zander founded the German Women's Order and members helped the SA with
soup kitchens and nursing services. Gertrud Baumer took over the new National Socialist
Women's Organisation in 1931 and it took control of women's societies after the Nazis
came to power. By 1934 women's organisations across Germany had been coordinated
and it was time invite the Reich Woman's Leader, Gertrud Scholtz-Klink, to speak to the
Reich Women's League.

Gertrud Scholtz-Klink (1902–1999)

Scholtz-Klink's first husband had died, leaving her with six children. Two of their children
had also died and she struggled to raise the others before she married for a second time
and had another five children. She had been a Nazi associate member since the early days
and she was the women's leader in Baden from 1929. Although Scholtz-Klink was an energetic worker and an effective organiser, she was expected to be a role model for German
women above all as a mother of a large family.

8

THE RALLY PROGRAMME

The Nuremberg Rally was a week-long festival of march pasts, torch light parades, speeches, fireworks and military displays. The following is an example of the scale and range of meetings and parades visitors would experience, based on the 1935 and 1936 rally programmes. Each organisation arranged meetings across the city where their leaders explained their plans to the senior delegates. Meanwhile, outdoor parades and military manoeuvres were arranged to keep the rank and file entertained.

Hitler believed that one of the main functions of the Congress was to explain his vision for the Third Reich and get his ideas across to the Party members. While the officials came to the stage and gave their speeches, the delegates listened; but there were no question and answer sessions. The Nazi regime was, after all, a dictatorship. The delegates were expected to pass on the Party messages to their local members when they returned home.

DAY 1: THE DAY OF GREETING

- Hitler arrived by train at Nuremberg Station.

- Press Reception in the House of Culture at 3:30pm with Dr Otto Dietrich, Reich Press Chief.

- Nuremberg's churches rang their bells at 5:30pm to open the Party Congress.

- Reception for Party leaders and government officials in Nuremberg City Hall at 6:00pm. Nuremberg Mayor Liebel introduces the Führer.

- Performance of Richard Wagner's 'Die Meistersinger von Nürnberg' began at the Nuremberg Opera House at 7:30pm; it lasted over four hours.

The SS guard of honour greet Hitler at Nuremberg station.

DAY 2: THE OPENING OF THE CONGRESS

- Opening ceremony in the Congress Hall at 11:00am with speakers:

  > Rudolf Hess, Deputy Party Leader
  > Julius Streicher, Franconian Gauleiter
  > Adolf Wagner, Bavarian Gauleiter
  > Viktor Lutze, SA Chief of Staff

- Cultural meeting at the Nuremberg Opera House at 8:00pm with Adolf Hitler and Alfred Rosenberg, Commissar for the Supervision of Intellectual and Ideological Education.

DAY 3: THE REICH LABOUR SERVICE DAY

Over 70,000 spectators filled the Zeppelin Field grandstand and terraces to watch the Reich Labour Service Rally, starting at 10.00am. Meanwhile, 45,000 labourers armed with shovels waited to the south of the stadium for the rally to begin. Cheers to the north signified that Hitler's motorcade was making its way through the crowds to the arena and the noise reached fever pitch as it pulled up in front of the speaker's podium.

The Reich Labour Service march past the Führer and the Zeppelin Tribune.

As soon as Hitler had taken his position next to his car, the first Reich Labour Service units began marching into the arena, in ranks eighteen men wide. They marched in through the south gate, passed in front of the Führer, and marched out through the north gate. Rows then doubled up and marched back into the arena through the west gate, deploying in their appointed positions. It did not take long for the stadium to fill up and as the last units passed the podium the Führer took his place on the platform alongside Reich Labour Leader Konstantin Hierl. The final units to enter the arena belonged to Labour Service schools. The men were stripped to the waist and took their place in front of the main stand before Hierl introduced his men to the Führer.

The standard bearers then moved into position as the men chanted slogans and sang songs; the standards were then dipped as the gathered assembly remembered those who had died in the war and the martyrs who had died fighting for the Party. Speeches by

Rudolf Hess introduces the Führer to the delegates.

Reich Labour Service leader Konstantin Hierl and Hitler brought the Reich Labour Service rally to an end.

- Part 1 of the Party Congress in Luitpold Hall at 5:30pm with speakers:

  > Alfred Rosenberg, Commissar for the Supervision of Intellectual and Ideological Education
  > Adolf Wagner, Bavarian Gauleiter
  > Walter Darré, Reich Minister of Food and Agriculture

This was first of five meetings in the Luitpold Hall. Party delegates gathered at the south west corner of the Luitpold Arena, looking up at the swastika flags draped from Speer's new concrete façade. Once inside, they took their seats and waited for the ceremony to begin. A huge swastika flag was hung from the far wall, forming a backdrop to the spectacle, while Hitler's personal banner had pride of place on the podium.

As the time drew near, senior officials walked down the hall and took their places on one of the 600 seats on elevated seating area facing the delegates. The suspense was broken by a fanfare of music and a parade of standard bearers marched to the front of the hall, taking up their positions at the back of the stage. Once they were all in position, Hitler and his body guard entered the hall.

The Führer took his place, flanked by Rudolf Hess and Julius Streicher on one side and Victor Lutze and Heinrich Himmler on the other. Senior Party officials including Franz Schwarz, Dr Robert Ley, Joseph Goebbels and Wilhelm Frick stood alongside while Hitler's adjutant, Julius Schaub, was always at his master's shoulder. Then the speeches began.

In the evening thousands of delegates marched along Frauentorgraben, the main road that ran outside Nuremberg's ancient city walls in a torch-lit parade. Hitler's hotel and Nuremberg's Opera House were on the opposite side of the road. The street was filled with the sounds of cheers and the smell of burning as the torch smoke filled the air.

The torchlight procession makes its way past Hitler's hotel.

DAY 4: THE DAY OF THE POLITICAL ORGANISATIONS

The day began with four early morning meetings around the city.

- Organisation for Ideological Indoctrination at the Opera House with speakers:

  Alfred Rosenberg, Commissar for the Supervision of Intellectual and Ideological Education
  Dr Robert Ley, head of the German Labour Front
  Max Frauendorfer, head of the General Government's Labour Division

- Association of National Socialist Jurists at the House of Culture with speakers:

  Julius Streicher, Franconia's Gauleiter
  Hans Frank, Reich Minister of Justice and head of the Party's Law Division
  Dr Ludwig Fischer, President of the Academy of German Law

- National Socialist Students Association in the Katherine Building with Alfred Rosenberg, Commissar for the Supervision of Intellectual and Ideological Education.

- Overseas (*Auslands*) Organisation for ex-patriots at the Apollo Theatre with speakers:

  Rudolf Hess, Deputy Party Leader
  Gauleiter Ernst Bohle, Head of the Overseas Organisation
  Paul Klemp, Head of the Overseas Organisation's shipping

- Part 2 of the Party Congress in Luitpold Hall at 10:30am with speakers:

  Joseph Goebbels, Reich Minister of Propaganda and Enlightenment
  Dr Robert Ley, head of the German Labour Front
  Erich Hilgenfeldt, of the People's Welfare Organisation and Winter Support Programme

Three afternoon meetings took place around the city.

- The National Socialist Press Association at the City Hall with speakers:

  Otto Dietrich; Reich Press Chief
  Helmut Sündermann, Dietrich's assistant
  Horst Dressler-Andrees, head of the Reich Radio Division

- The Committee on Finance and Administration at City Hall with the following speakers:

  Franz Schwarz, NSDAP Treasurer
  Hans Saupert, Reich Audit Department

Joseph 'Sepp' Dietrich (standing left in the background) headed the Führer's security team.

- The War Victims Welfare Service at the House of Culture with speakers:

   Willy Liebel, Nuremberg Mayor
   Hanns Oberlindober, head of the War Victims Welfare Service

The Political Leaders Rally

As the sun set, 90,000 Party members marched through the streets of Nuremberg, cheered along by massive crowds. They were led onto Zeppelin Field by hundreds of standard bearers and as the sky darkened the stage show began. A single floodlight shot a beam of light into the night sky; then lights illuminated the main stand, its white stone gleaming against the night sky. Lights then lit up the entire arena.

As the leaders gathered on the grandstand, 500 pupils of the Vogelsang Order Castle choir (from the elite youth academy) took their place in front of the speaker's podium. The grandstand lights were switched off, plunging the front of the arena into darkness. As a hush fell over the crowd, Dr Robert Ley announced the Führer's imminent arrival and as the motorcade roared into the arena, the lights were switched on again while Hitler walked to the speaker's podium. Standard bearers entered through the stadium entrances and spotlights picked out the main ones while they took their place. All the time bugle fanfares declared the ceremony open.

90,000 delegates could cram into the Zeppelin Field to hear their Führer.

Dr Ley salutes Hitler during the Rally of the Political Leaders.

The choir opened the oath ceremony and Party members reiterated their promise to serve the Führer and the Party. Standards then dipped as the assembled crowds honoured the war dead and Party martyrs. They rose again before Dr Robert Ley read the second part of the oath. The Führer's speech was the highlight of the ceremony and he reminded everyone of what they had achieved so far and what the future held.

The German Women's League Rally

The area around Luitpold Hall was filled with colour as members of German Women's League gathered for their evening rally and took their seats inside. Many women were dressed in their traditional regional costumes, providing a contrast to the drab uniforms worn by the men. The hall was full two hours before the meeting opened and thousands of women who could not get a seat gathered in Luitpold Arena to listen to the proceedings over loudspeakers.

The tension was broken when shouts of 'Heil' greeted the Führer, Reich Women's Leader, Frau Gertrud Scholtz-Klink, and Erich Hilgenfeldt, head of the Reich Welfare Organisation and Winter Support Programme. As they took their seats, a short piece by the Reich Symphony Orchestra was followed by a greeting by Hilgenfeldt. Sixteen thousand women then rose to their feet to sing.

Scholtz-Klink made the first speech, explaining the woman's role in the National Socialist state. Hitler explained that women had to serve their husbands and raise their children to help the State. He explained how the school system and the German Girls League were educating the mothers of the future.

Scholtz-Klink brought the meeting to a close by promising the Führer that the German Women's League was dedicated to achieving his goals. The assembly then stood for a final song and the reaffirmation of their oath to serve the Führer ended the rally. Hitler then faced the huge crowds waiting outside.

DAY 5: THE HITLER YOUTH DAY

Meeting of the Central Administration Office at 8:00am in St Katherine's Church.

Review of the Hitler Youth in the Municipal Stadium

Starting in the early morning, endless columns of Hitler Youth units marched from Langwasser camp into the Franken Stadium and while the majority paraded on the sports field, others took their places in the grandstands. While the choirs and musical groups faced the stadium platform, navy units paraded to the left and right of the platform.

Long before Hitler was due at 10:00am, 50,000 members of the Hitler Youth were in their places waiting for drummers and buglers on the timber watchtowers to announce the arrival of the guests of honour. Reich Leaders Max Amann, Martin Bormann, Walter Buch, Alfred Rosenberg, Dr Robert Ley, Dr Otto Dietrich and the Gauleiters represented

The Hitler Youth wait expectantly for the Führer's arrival in the Franken Stadium.

the Party. The three military leaders, Reich Minister General Göring of the Luftwaffe, General Fritsch of the Army and Admiral Raeder of the Navy, represented the Wehrmacht, while SA Chief of Staff, Ernst Röhm (Victor Lutze after 1934) and Reichsführer-SS Heinrich Himmler represented their organisations. Other military leaders, party and state officials and diplomatic bureaucrats sat behind.

A loud command alerted the assembly and everyone stood to attention as the Führer's motorcade entered the stadium. Loud cheers virtually drowned out the fanfare of bugles as Hitler and Reich Minister Rudolf Hess walked between the lines of SS guards to the podium followed by Reich Youth Leader Baldur von Schirach and his chief of staff.

Once they reached the stage, silence fell across the crowd as Schirach opened the rally and introduced the Führer to the Hitler Youth, many of them who had never seen him before. To be one of the chosen few to attend the rally was a great privilege and they returned the Führer's greeting 'Heil, my youth' with a hearty 'Heil Hitler'. Then a blare of trumpets announced the beginning of the ceremony as the assembly sang the first of many songs.

A young announcer read the formal introduction to the Führer and as a second, slower song began, Hitler Youth standards entered the stadium led by the Herbert Norkus standard (it honoured a young Nazi martyr killed by Communists in February 1932). The standards had been carried from their headquarters across Germany, on the great Adolf-Hitler-March, the Hitler Youth's contribution to raising support for the rally. A third song filled in the time as the bearers found their place.

Schirach then stepped forward and introduced the crowd to Hitler, detailing their achievements and the enthusiasm and hard work required to make them happen. Cheers marked the end of the speech and a hush fell over the crowd as Hitler began to speak. He explained his vision for the immediate and long term future of Germany and the Hitler Youth's part in it achieving it. When his speech ended, a command silenced the cheers and the young men and boys stood to attention ready for the inspection parade.

A drum rhythmically beat out a slow march as the Führer left the stage and walked along the endless ranks. More songs followed but the highlight for many, particularly those at the back of the stands, was when the Führer was driven slowly around the running track. The motorcade left the stadium as the boys sang the Hitler Youth anthem, but the cheers continued long after Hitler was out of earshot. Yet again the Führer had reaffirmed his connection with a selection of Germany's male youth; they in turn had had an unforgettable experience.

- Meeting of the Labour Front in the Luitpold Hall, starting at 11:30am with speakers:

  Adolf Hitler, the Führer
  Dr Robert Ley, head of the German Labour Front

The Führer is driven around the stadium to get close to the Hitler Youth.

Hjalamr Schacht, Reich Minister of Economics
Franz Seldte, Reich Minister for Labour
Rudolf Schmeer, assistant secretary of the Reich Minister of Economics

- Meeting of the Welfare Organisation at the House of Culture starting at 12:00 noon with speakers:

Erich Hilgenfeldt, head of the Reich People's Welfare and Winter Help Programme
Hermann Althaus, head of the Reich Youth Welfare Department
Mayerhofer and Laemme (unknown speakers)

- Part 3 of the Party Congress in Luitpold Hall, starting at 3:00pm with speakers:

Max Amann, head of the Reich Press Chamber
Fritz Todt, Inspector-General of the Road and Highway System
Hans Frank, Reich Minister of Justice and head of the Party's Law Division

DAY 6: THE DAY OF THE SS AND THE SA

Parade of the SS and the SA on Luitpold Arena

Units were allocated times for ablutions and feeding to prevent extensive queuing at the facilities on Langwasser Camp and the first bugle calls started around 2.00am; they continued for several hours until everyone was roused. After washing, men queued for breakfast at the Bavarian Relief Train by the entrance to the camp (it was situated outside the Mars Field Station in 1938). It was a huge facility, one to rival any mobile military kitchen, and the cooking teams prepared tens of thousands of meals every day.

After breakfast, units formed up in their staging area ready to march to the event; the parades through the old town centre involved the longest march. The nature of the rallies was that different units had to be in different arenas at different times; it meant that thousands of men were marching to and from the tent city all day long.

Over 150,000 SS and SA men assembled in Luitpold Arena along with detachments of the National Socialist Motor Corps (NSKK) and the National Socialist Flying Corps (NSFK). Everyone had to be in their place ready for an 8:00am start. They paraded on the huge grassed area, leaving a wide gap in the centre, so that the Nazi leaders could look across to the Hall of Honour. The grass strip was covered in granite slabs in time for the 1934 rally.

Standard bearers then took their places either side of the monument and at the given signal a hush fell over the crowd while Hitler marched across the centre of the arena with Ernst Röhm, the head of the SA to the Hall of Honour. While Röhm played a key role in the ceremony until 1933, he was murdered following his arrest on the Night of the Long Knives on 30 June 1934. In September 1934 Victor Lutze was joined by Reichführer-SS Heinrich Himmler. The arena remained silent while the three men paused before a huge wreath and then saluted the war dead and the Nazi martyrs.

Lutze and Himmler flank Hitler as he salutes the Hall of Honour.

The Blood Flag ceremony.

The leaders then retraced their steps across the arena followed by Jakob Grimminger carrying the Blood Flag (*Blutfahne*), the tattered Swastika flag carried by the 5th SA Sturm during the 1923 Munich Putsch. Legend has it that the flag was torn and spattered with blood during the uprising. It was then either hidden by the flag bearer, Heinrich Trambauer, or confiscated by the police. Either way, it ended up in the hands of Karl Eggers and was then kept at the Brown House (*Braunes Haus*), the Nazi Party headquarters in Munich (if indeed what was at the rally was the original Munich flag at all).

As the three leaders mounted the stand, Grimminger took his place behind, ready for the dedication of unit flags. SS units then filled the centre of the Luitpold Arena. As solemn music played, Hitler passed along the line of standards clutching the Blood Flag in one hand, while seizing each new flag in turn, a quasi-religious ceremony.

The units then left the arena and marched to their staging area in the St Lorenz district, ready for the city centre march past.

March Past through Adolf Hitler Platz

Nuremberg's castle sits on top a hill, looking down on the city. At the foot of the hill is Hauptmarkt, where the Church of Our Lady (*Frauenkirche*) stands over the large square used as a focal point during the early rallies. Stands were erected around the edge of the square for the crowds while Hitler stood in a car surrounded by his closest followers, including Rudolf Hess, Hermann Göring and Ernst Röhm (Victor Lutze after 1934). Jakob Grimminger stood with the Blood Flag behind the car. The car stood next to one of Nuremberg's landmarks, the Beautiful Fountain (*Schöner Brunnen*), a replica of a late fourteenth-century structure.

The square was renamed Adolf-Hitler-Platz in 1933 and while the parade remained the same it took longer and longer each year. All morning SA and SS units gathered south of the River Pegnitz, waiting their turn to march past their Führer. The first ones set off at 11:30am and crossed the river via Fleisch Bridge, or Meat Bridge, a wide sixteenth-century structure. They entered the square with the cheers of the crowds ringing in their ears and then, with arms raised in the Nazi salute, it was eyes right as they marched past the Führer's entourage. The march continued up the hill past St Sebaldus Church on the left and the Town Hall to the right and ended in front of the castle gates at the top of the hill. After all the build-up and excitement, the troops faced a long march back to their campsite.

- Part 4 of the Party Congress in Luitpold Hall, starting at 6:00pm with speakers:

  Fritz Reinhardt, State Secretary in the Finance Ministry
  Dr Otto Dietrich, Reich Press Chief
  Konstantin Hierl, Reich Labour Leader

- Session of the Reichstag at the House of Culture starting at 6:00pm with speakers:

  Hermann Göring, President of the Reichstag
  Adolf Hitler, the Führer

SA units march
past the Führer's
entourage in
Adolf-Hitler-Platz.

DAY 7 (AFTER 1938): THE DAY OF THE COMMUNITY

The Day of the Community was added to the rally in 1938 and it consisted of a series
of massed athletic exhibitions on the Zeppelin Field. Men from different organisations
performed gymnastic exercises with medicine balls and tree trunks. Women from the Faith
and Beauty organisation then demonstrated exercises based upon folk dancing. The purpose of the displays was to demonstrate the advantages of a healthy, energetic lifestyle.

Young women perform physical exercises in the Franken Stadium.

THE FINAL DAY: THE ARMED FORCES DAY

The day of the armed forces on the Zeppelin Field proved to be the highlight of the rally for the Party rank and file. Around 70,000 spectators attended each display, all eager to see the army and air force in action. Its popularity was reflected in the higher admission charges. While the organisers charged two Reichmarks on the side stands and ten Reichmarks on the main stand, they only charged one and three Reichmarks for the same seats during the Reich Labour Service parade. Two military displays were held, one in the morning and one in the afternoon, doubling the number of people who could see the show; it also doubled the gate receipts.

The morning display was opened by the Minister of War, Field Marshal von Blomberg, and he was joined on the platform by the army, navy and air force commanders.

Proceedings opened at 9:00am while Hitler and senior Party leaders attended one of eight meetings across the city (full details of the armed forces display are given below).

- NSDAP political leadership at the Nuremberg Opera House:
     Rudolf Hess, Deputy Party Leader

- Propaganda officials at the Apollo Theatre:
     Joseph Goebbels, Reich Minister of Propaganda and Enlightenment

- The Committee on Agrarian Policies at the Katherine Building:
     Walter Darré, Reich Minister of Food and Agriculture

- The Economic Policies Committee at the House of Culture:
     Bernhard Koehler; Economist
     Schaub (perhaps Julius Schaub, Hitler's personal adjutant)

- The Committee for Industry at the City Hall:
     Fritz Todt, Inspector-General of the Road and Highway System
     Oskar Staebel, head of the National Socialist Association for Technology
     Fruth (unknown role)
     Georg Seebauer, director of the Office of Technology

- The National Socialist Jurists Association at the City Hall:
     Hans Frank, Reich Minister of Justice and head of the Party's Law Division
     Dr Ludwig Fischer, President of the Academy of German Law

- The Committee for Community Policies at the Congress Hall:
     Johannes Weidemann, Bürgermeister of Halle
     Karl Fiehler, Bürgermeister of Munich
     Hanns Kerrl, Reich Minister for Church Affairs

- The National Socialist Teachers' Association at the Apollo Theatre:
     Julius Streicher, Gauleiter of Franconia
     Kolb (unknown role)

The Second Wehrmacht Display

Hitler attended the 2.00pm demonstration and Field Marshal von Blomberg once again opened the proceedings on the Zeppelin Field. The show began with a march past by 45,000 men and unit after unit paraded along the road in front of the grandstand. While the Party leaders enjoyed the show, the crowds were eager to see the military display.

Faces turned upwards at the sound of approaching aeroplanes as reconnaissance planes and then fighter squadrons flew in formation 100 metres above the arena. The pilots

Infantry stage attacks in the Zeppelin Arena.

Panzer I and Panzer II tanks drive through the Zeppelin Arena.

returned to perform crowd pleasing stunts before flying into the distance. Attention then turned to the arena as halftracks towed anti-aircraft guns into the stadium and their crews prepared for action. Dive bombers made bombing runs over the arena while light anti-aircraft batteries returned blank fire. As the dive bombers headed off, heavy bombers made bombing runs while the heavy anti-aircraft 'returned fire'. As soon as the air demonstration came to an end the gun crews limbered up and the anti-aircraft guns left the arena. A fly past by all the planes brought the Luftwaffe demonstration to an end.

Horsemen with trumpets announced the next part of the show; a parade of cavalry units. 1000 horsemen entered the stadium by the three gates and formed up in front of the main grandstand. They then left the arena in tight formation.

After the controlled cavalry parade, the crowds cheered as horse teams cantered into the arena pulling light artillery guns. As the horses came to a halt in the middle of the arena, the gun crews took their positions and fired salvoes. They then limbered up and left as quickly as they had entered.

As reconnaissance cavalry troops entered the arena, a red flare announced that the battle was about to begin. Everyone was eager to see the army's new tanks but the display was all about demonstrating how modern mobile troops worked together. While the cavalry scouts deployed and hunted down the enemy, anti-tank guns and machine gun teams deployed and opened fire. At the same time, signal troops relayed the progress of the battle to the approaching armour.

The Luftwaffe fly over the Zeppelin Arena.

A motorised reconnaissance unit entered the arena and began spotting the enemy positions on the opposite side of the arena for an artillery unit. Tanks then roared in, weaving back and forth demonstrating their speed and manoeuvrability. They ended the demonstration by stopping in lines in front of the main grandstand and fired a closing salvo. As the tanks left, an artillery unit deployed in the arena and the crews erected camouflage over their guns before firing salvos. At the same time signal men deployed behind the guns and displayed their skills.

The last part of the display was a large mock battle designed to demonstrate combined arms tactics. Despite the small size of the arena, machine gun teams and light artillery deployed behind barbed wire entanglements and a mock minefield as the 'enemy'. 'Friendly' infantry then entered the arena and began advancing towards the enemy position while artillery deployed and opened fire. But the first attack failed and as the infantry fell back, tank

The night-time military display brings the Rally to a close for another year.

reinforcements entered the arena to save the day. The first wave advanced as far as the enemy position and although many were disabled by the minefield, the second wave crushed the barbed wire and occupied the enemy position. The battle ended with the infantry reinforcing the tanks. Between them, the infantry, tanks and artillery had won the day.

With the battle over, the organisers prepared the Zeppelin Field for the final parade. As soon as the arena was clear, 18,000 servicemen marched in through the three gates and formed up in front of the main grandstand army, navy and air force units parading from right to left. Cavalry units, motorised units, artillery, anti-tank, flak, signal and tank units deployed behind the foot troops.

Once everyone was in position the ceremony began with every officer drawing his dagger. As the band struck up with the 'Frederick the Great March,' standard bearers marched into the arena. The flags of the old army led the parade while the new Wehrmacht flags followed and they all paraded before the main platform. As the song came to an end General Field Marshall von Blomberg spoke to the assembled soldiers and the crowds. The band then played the 'Presentation March' while General Freiherr von Fritsch awarded flags to army units, Admiral Raeder awarded flags to navy units and General Göring awarded flags to Luftwaffe units.

As the demonstration came to a close the crowds joined the servicemen in the singing of the national anthem. A group of 17 planes then flew over the arena in a swastika formation, drawing gasps from the crowds; the airship *Hindenburg* also flew overhead. The last song of the event was the Party's anthem, the *Horst Wessel Lied* (also known as 'The Flag on High' or *Die Fahne Hoch*). The display came to an end with the military units marching out of the arena while the crowds dispersed.

- Final Part of the Party Congress in Luitpold Hall at 6:30pm with the following speakers:

    Rudolf Hess, Deputy Party Leader
    Adolf Hitler

- The final parade was a night-time military tattoo on the Zeppelin Field.

- A midnight flag-lowering ceremony in front of the Führer's hotel closed the Party Congress.

9

PRESENTING THE RALLIES TO THE PEOPLE

While tens of thousands attended the Nuremberg rallies each year, millions of Germans could not. The Nazis wanted their message to spread as far as possible and they took steps to make permanent records of the events, both oral and visual. In the 1930s the main media forms were radio, newsreels and newspapers. All three were exploited to the maximum. After 1933 the State Broadcasting Company (*Reichs-Rundfunk-Gesellschaft* or RRG) made radio broadcasts and movie companies distributed newsreels to cinemas across the country. Leni Reifensthal also made full-length films of the rallies. A variety of souvenirs were put on sale, ranging from picture books to postcards and from posters to uniforms.

BROADCASTING THE RALLIES

The State Broadcasting Company was established when Germany's regional companies were merged in 1925. As soon as the Nazis seized power the company was nationalised and used extensively by Dr Joseph Goebbels' Ministry of Public Enlightenment and Propaganda; by April 1934 all remaining broadcasting companies across the country had been taken over.

Radio was one of the main ways of communicating with the masses in the 1930s and Goebbels knew that spoken propaganda was more powerful than the written version, as did Hitler. Goebbels also knew that many German families relied on their radio for the news. The Nazis subsidised cheap People's Receivers so that families could afford one and by 1939 70 per cent of households owned a set.

Radio was also the best way to provide live coverage of the rallies and Reich transmission conductor Eugene Hadamovsky established a team of commentators and technicians in Nuremberg's telegraph office, in Allersberger Strasse, next to the railway station. The rallies were the largest outside broadcasts attempted by Rundfunk and by 1937 it had 64 engineers and technicians working with five outside broadcasting vans. They all worked together to broadcast live transmissions across the Reich.

A relaxed Hitler listens to a radio broadcast.

In 1937 Hitler Youth Groups and Reich Labour Service units were earmarked to erect column speakers in urban public spaces to get radio transmissions to the public. The plan was to establish a network of 6600 Reich speakers but only a pilot project of 100 had been completed in Breslau by the time Germany invaded Poland.

Between them Goebbels and Hadamovsky drew up a tightly controlled programme schedule to ensure blanket coverage of the rallies. As well as live broadcasts, two hours of reports started at 8.00pm each night. A mixture of dance and folk music and military marches were mixed in with the speeches to keep listeners tuned in.

Hadamovsky brought together experienced commentators from across Germany, ones who brought a sense of suspense and excitement to the narrative and they relied on a specially printed source book to provide information on the parades and personalities. The commentaries were also mixed with interviews, speeches and marching music to hold the listeners' attention.

Minister of Public Enlightenment and Propaganda

Dr Joseph Goebbels (1897–1945) was rejected for army service in the First World War because of a crippled foot and he turned to education, completing a doctorate in philology at Heidelberg by 1921. He joined the NSDAP in 1922 and moved to the Ruhr district to work as editor of the *Volkische Freiheit* (People's Freedom) newspaper. He also became business manager for the North Rhineland Gau, editing Gregor Strasser's publications.

Goebbels stands between General Blomberg and Generalfeldmarshall Göring.

Goebbels switched his allegiance to Hitler after the Bamberg Party Conference in February 1926 and was appointed Gauleiter for Berlin-Brandenburg. He used his newspaper *Der Angriff* (The Assault) to raise the Party's profile and attack political opponents.

Goebbels was a talented speaker and propaganda expert who adapted American advertising techniques for the NSDAP. He introduced the 'Heil Hitler!' greeting between Party members and turned the murdered SA trooper, Horst Wessel, into a martyr promoting his song, *Horst Wesel Lied*, as the official party anthem. In May 1928, Goebbels was elected Berlin representative for the Reichstag and the following year he was appointed the NSDAP's Head of Propaganda and revitalised the Party campaigns, becoming one of Hitler's most influential advisers.

Goebbels was appointed Reich Minister for Public Enlightenment and Propaganda in March 1933 giving him a huge influence over all aspects of German life. He had a close interest in the Germany's film industry, and promoted both radio and television as propaganda tools. In 1933 he encouraged the manufacture of an affordable radio set which could only receive German stations and two years later he launched a limited television service in Berlin.

Director of National Radio Programming
Euden Hadamovsky (1904–1945) was a Berliner and early Nazi supporter who specialised in radio broadcasts. Shortly after the Nazi takeover Hans Bredow was forced to resign as

National Programming Director for refusing to adhere to the regime's policy on broadcasting. Hadamovsky was his replacement and dealt with many of the technical issues related to broadcasting from the rallies. He was also an expert on propaganda, writing seven books on the subject, including 'Propaganda and National Power' in 1933. While Hadamovsky did not get on with Goebbels, he was appointed chief of staff of the NSDAP's Central Propaganda Office in 1942. He served on the Eastern Front with the 4th Polizei Division after 1944 as an Obersturmführer and was killed in action in March 1945.

NEWSREELS AND TELEVISION

Newsreels were popular in the 1930s and many people headed to the cinema to experience a visual record of the news. Crews from Ufa, Deulig, Tobis and Fox were given access to all areas of the rallies to make short newsreel films that were shipped to cinemas around the Reich. Some were shipped abroad to German ex-pat communities around the world.

In 1935 the Nazis announced the world's first television company. However, technology was primitive and while the cameras could stream live film they had no facilities for saving or repeating footage. Viewers could only watch the broadcasts in one of the few television parlours set up in Party offices around Berlin and Potsdam. The first live outside broadcast was made from the 1936 Olympics in Berlin and it is believed around 1000 viewers watched live footage from the 1937 Nuremberg Rally.

A movie camera team films Hitler's entourage as they return to his hotel.

The television headquarters were set up in Nuremberg's telegraph office during the rally and technicians switched the transmission between cameras working with the outside broadcast vans. Plans for a private television channel in Nuremberg were abandoned when war broke out. While the limited exposure of television did not have the impact of the newsreels or Riefenstahl's film, a select few had experienced the future of marketing.

FILMING THE RALLIES

The first official film about a Party rally was made in 1927, soon after the opening of the NSDAP film office. However, the film maker who will always be associated with the Nuremberg Rallies is Leni Riefenstahl and she directed three documentary films in 1933, 1934 and 1935.

Leni Riefenstahl was a popular German actress, who was impressed by Hitler. The Führer was equally impressed when he watched her first attempt at directing, 'The Blue Light' (*Das Blaue Licht*), in 1932. By the summer of 1933 many Germans knew little about what happened in Nurembrg and the decision was taken to make a film about the September rally to spread the Party message.

Hitler pressed Riefenstahl to direct the film and she eventually agreed only a couple of weeks before the rally. The late decision left little time to assemble a crew or prepare for the filming but Riefenstahl's main problem was that she had to film around the rally,

Victor Lutze, head of the SA after 1934, Hitler and Leni Riefenstahl.

rather than the rally being staged for filming. Outdoor filming of the parades proved to be a challenge and it did not help that Hitler hated being filmed. Goebbels also objected to the idea, especially when his demands to release the film through the Propaganda Ministry were ignored.

The film was called 'The Victory of Faith' (*Der Sieg des Glaubens*) and it was well received at the box office despite its substandard quality. It had not been in circulation long when Ernst Röhm, head of the SA, was murdered following the Night of the Long Knives on 30 June 1934. His image was banned and as he had played a leading role in the rally, all copies had to be withdrawn and virtually all were destroyed.

After all the problems filming the 1933 rally, Riefenstahl recommended fellow director Walter Ruttmann for the next one. Ruttmann wanted to make a history of the rise of the NSDAP starting in 1923 and ending with the 1934 Nuremberg Rally but Hitler was against the idea. He preferred Riefenstahl's approach and wanted her to do it again, only this time she would have more time, more support and no interference from the Propaganda Ministry. This time the rally was planned around the propaganda film, involving close cooperation amongst Hitler, Speer and Riefenstahl. Riefenstahl was able to make a far superior film thanks to a large budget, extensive preparations, and support from high-ranking Nazis.

Hitler and Leni Riefenstahl discuss the film.

The title was the 'Triumph of the Will' (*Triumph des Willens*), named after the 'Rally of the Will' (or maybe the other way round), and as 'Victory of Faith' had been consigned to the cutting room floor, Riefenstahl was able to use a similar script, repeating many scenes and camera angles. Composer Herbert Windt also reused parts of the musical score.

One of Albert Speer's responsibilities was to create a low-cost visual spectacle for the rallies using temporary props, particularly swastika flags, to enhance the permanent structures. He worked alongside Riefenstahl, finding exciting camera angles and then incorporated features for the film crews. Pits were dug in front of the speakers' platform for the low angle shots while elevators on the huge flags were used for high-angle shots. Tracks were laid in many places so the camera crews could make travelling shots.

This time Riefenstahl had a large crew of 172 people to work with and many dressed in SA uniforms so they blended into the crowds; 36 cameramen and assistants worked in 16 teams, most of them using two cameras, while 27 technical and lighting men worked together to produce a film of high quality. Nine aerial photographers captured overhead sequences while two photographers took stills; 29 newsreel men compiled useful information. Riefenstahl's artistic teams were supported by 37 security personnel, 26 drivers, four labourers and two office assistants.

Leni Riefenstahl takes her seat for the premiere of 'Victory of Faith'.

A film crew follows Hitler as he starts his march across Luitpold Arena.

The film crews used new techniques, such as moving cameras, long focus lenses to create a distorted perspective, and aerial photography. Riefenstahl and Windt worked closely together to create an innovative combination of film and music. The problems of outdoor broadcasting were overcome by allowing speakers to reread their speeches if the sound quality was poor.

Riefenstahl worked hard to complete the editing on time, condensing over 60 hours of footage into 104 minutes for her exacting client. 'The Triumph of the Will' premiered at the Berlin Ufa Palace Theatre on 28 March 1935 and it was a great success across Germany. It earned 815,000 Reichsmarks in the first two months alone, making it into the top three of German-made films of 1934.

The film was well received by Party officials, compared to the reception of 'Victory of Faith' but several generals raised objections over the limited amount of footage covering the Day of the Wehrmacht. Poor weather was one factor but while there was extensive coverage of the SS, the SA and the Reich Labour Service, there was only one military orientated scene, a review of German cavalry units. Hitler wanted to appease the generals by introducing a new scene but Riefenstahl refused to compromise. Instead she returned to Nuremberg in 1935 to make a short film about the Wehrmacht, called 'Day of Freedom: Our Wehrmacht' (*Tag der Freiheit: Unsere Wehrmacht*). A short 21-minute film called 'Festive Nuremberg' (*Festliches Nürnberg*) covered the highlights of the 1936 and 1937 rallies.

Despite the objections from the military, Riefenstahl was awarded the German Film Prize, a gold medal at the 1935 Venice Biennale, and the Grand Prix award at the 1937 World Exhibition in Paris. Although the film was not promoted heavily outside Germany, it won awards in the United States, France, Sweden, and other countries.

Leni Riefenstahl is sometimes referred to as the greatest female filmmaker of the twentieth century, even though she only directed eight films, of which just two were popular outside of Germany. After the war she was imprisoned for four years for being a Nazi sympathiser and was permanently blacklisted by the film industry. She always maintained that she was not a Nazi, just a film director working for the government of the day. Riefenstahl died in 2003 and her obituaries reaffirmed the importance of 'Triumph of the Will' as an important historical example of propaganda cinematography.

Although the film is well known, the content is not. The endless black and white images of parades and Nazi leaders making speeches can be tedious. While the future in store for Germany and the rest of Europe was not known at the time, it is chilling to see people cheering on the men who initiated the Second World War and planned the Holocaust. It is still possible to purchase copies of the film while the internet provides excerpts. What follows is a brief rundown of the fourteen scenes of the 110 minutes of film.

TRIUMPH OF THE WILL (*TRIUMPH DES WILLENS*) SCRIPT OVERVIEW

Musical introduction and credits.
>   *On 5 September 1934…*
>   *20 years after the outbreak of the World War…*

16 years after the beginning of German suffering...
19 months after the beginning of the German rebirth...
Adolf Hitler flew again to Nuremberg to review the columns of his faithful followers...

Part 1: Hitler's Arrival in Nuremberg

The scene charts Hitler's flight over Nuremberg in a Junkers Ju52 plane as the SA marches below. Thousands are waiting at the airfield to get a glimpse of him before he is whisked away in his motorcade. The film follows the Führer's drive through the crowded streets and ends at the Deustch Hof Hotel where he appears on the balcony.

Part 2: The Night Rally in front of Hitler's Hotel

Torches light up Hitler's hotel and while musicians play, the SS guards keep the crowds at bay.

Part 3: Early Morning over Nuremberg

As the sun rises over Nuremberg and the townspeople start another day, swastika flags are seen everywhere while the church bells ring. Meanwhile, everyone is stirring on the camping grounds, and preparing for the day's activities as the sound of trumpets takes over from church bells. Peasants in traditional costume line the streets hoping to catch a glimpse of Hitler and senior party officials as they leave for the Rally Grounds.

Himmler, Lutze, Hess and Hitler salute the delegates in Luitpold Hall.

'The Triumph of the Will'. In some ways the work was a triumph of Riefenstahl's will.

Part 4: Opening of the Reich Party Congress

Rudolf Hess opens the 6th Reich Party Congress in the Luitpold Hall, introducing the Führer to the delegates. Excerpts from the speeches made by Adolf Wagner, Alfred Rosenberg, Otto Dietrich, Fritz Todt, Fritz Reinhardt, Walter Darré, Julius Streicher, Robert Ley, Hans Frank, Dr Joseph Goebbels and Konstantin Hierl, follow.

Part 5: Reich Labour Service Day

Konstantin Hierl introduces thousands of members of the Reich Labour Service to the Führer on the Zeppelin Field. A group leader asks which area men are from and twelve individuals reply in turn, demonstrating that the crowd come from all over Germany. After pledging to work for Germany, Hitler reaffirms their purpose in the Third Reich.

Part 6: SA Night Rally

Viktor Lutze speaks to the SA on the Zeppelin Field. The torch-lit parade culminates in a bonfire and firework show.

Part 7: Hitler Youth Day Rally

There are scenes of anticipation as 50,000 members of the Hitler Youth watch the Führer's arrival in the Franken Stadium. Baldur von Schirach makes the introduction and then Hitler speaks. The sequence closes with Hitler being driven around the stadium in front of an enthusiastic crowd.

Part 8: Review of New Military Equipment

An evening review of new military vehicles held in the Zeppelin Field. Hitler and Hess are joined by Reich Minister of Aviation Göring, General von Blomberg representing the army and Admiral Raeder representing the navy.

Part 9: The Political Leaders' Rally

The night-time gathering of over 200,000 political leaders in the Zeppelin Field begins with standard bearers marching onto the parade ground. Hitler addresses the assembly and the sequence ends with them marching away from the stadium, many carrying torches.

Part 10: The Memorial Ceremony

The SS and the SA gather in Luitpold Arena in front of Hitler, Heinrich Himmler and Viktor Lutze. The three leaders walk across the centre of the arena and salute the war memorial.

Riefenstahl used a variety of camera angles to film 'Triumph of the Will'.

Part 11: The SA and SS Review and Rally

Hitler and Hess watch as around 200,000 members of the SA and the SS march into Luitpold Arena. Lutze introduces the rally and then Hitler addresses the crowd.

Part 12: The Blood Flag Ceremony

A single gun fires shots, announcing the start of the Blood Flag ceremony. Hitler holds the corner of the flag as he walks along a line of standards, shaking hands with the standard bearers; the gun continues to fire during the ceremony.

Part 13: The Outdoors Military Review of Third Reich Organisations

Hitler's motorcade drives through Nuremberg and he takes his place alongside Göring in Adolf-Hitler-Platz. Various organisations parade through the square in front of their respective leaders.

Part 14: The Party Congress Closing Ceremony

Party leaders and standard bearers enter Luitpold Hall and take their place on the platform. Hitler addresses an enthusiastic crowd followed by a closing speech by Hess. The assembly sings *Horst Wesel Lied* as the film comes to an end.

SOUVENIRS AND PHOTOGRAPHY

The tens of thousands of visitors to the Nuremberg Rallies were eager to take home souvenirs of their memorable visit. Souvenirs were particularly important for projecting the Party image during pre-television and internet days; they were also a valuable source of income. Souvenirs came in many forms, ranging from photographs and postcards to commemorative books and scrapbooks. They also came in different qualities ranging from the high standard Party offerings to low standard, unofficial products.

The pictures we usually see of the Nuremberg Rallies (including those used in this book) were taken by professional photographers, including Heinrich Hoffmann, Ludwig Harren and Lala Aufsberg. They were given access to the best vantage points so they could take top quality images of the parades and rallies. These photographers were also given access to speaker's podiums and other limited access areas so they could take close-up shots of the Party leaders. While the photographers wisely did not try to take embarrassing photographs, censors made sure that no awkward pictures slipped through the net.

Despite the tight rein on the professional photographers, the censors could do little about the thousands of visitors who took souvenir snapshots with their own cameras. These 'clickers' (the German slang name for amateur photographers) usually took photographs of the rally ground structures or shots of their comrades on the camping grounds. Private pictures were usually of a poor standard because were taken from difficult angles or

Only Hoffmann was allowed to take close ups of the Party leaders.

from a distance. Consequently, they were frowned on by the Nazi organisers because they showed the rallies at their rawest. Members of the Hitler Youth were given specific instructions about taking pictures: 'Photography is permitted only during free time in the camp. Cameras must not be taken into the stadium or they will be confiscated. Photographs of the stadium during the Saturday afternoon rally will be available at the stalls in the camp.'

Instead of taking photographs, visitors to the rallies were encouraged to buy official postcards, a favourite travel souvenir of the 1930s. Postcards could either be collected or sent home to friends and families to let them know they had arrived safely.

BOOKS AND PRINTED MATTER

There were two types of rally books. The 'Red Book' was the NSDAP's official publication and it contained a full run down of the rally along with transcripts of the speeches in chronological order. It also had a number of small photographs. The 'Blue Book' was published by Julius Streicher's Nuremberg publishing house, earning a great deal of revenue for the Franconian Gauleiter. The book was a larger format and it had a shortened version of the proceedings and excerpts from speeches. It had many more photographs and they were larger. The Blue Book was a tabloid version of the Red Book.

The symbols of the rally from 1935 through to 1939.

Heinrich Hoffman's photography company also published commemorative picture books and pamphlets of Hitler's speeches, raising more money for the Party. The picture books were an important record of the rally in pre-television days and the professional photographs of the Party leaders and parades were a still version of Riefenstahl's films.

Hoffman's early work in Munich, Nuremberg and Weimar was dull and uninspiring because he concentrated on the columns of marching men, to portray the growing support for the Party. His pictures improved after 1933 because the Rally Ground structures provided perfect backdrops for impressive photographs. Small companies and individual photographers also produced souvenir pictures books and while a few were professional products with artistic photographs, many were poor quality.

Children's Books and Poems

Two books for children were sold at the rallies. Franz Bauer wrote a story following a group of boys as they explored Nuremberg city and the Rally Grounds. It was an introduction to Nazi ideals for young men and the narrative and illustrations helped the young enquiring mind find out more. Nuremberg-based writer Anna Liebel-Monninger wrote a story for girls in which young Gertrude falls in love, gets married and raises a family, all with the Reich Party Congress as a background. It, too, was an introduction to the Nazis' ideals, but for young women.

Local poet Paul Riess, who wrote under the pseudonym Pausala, composed a poem about a jolly character's visit to Nuremberg called 'Holidays in Dear Old Nuremberg' (*Festtage im lieben alten Nürnberg*). It was a naive piece and Riess even chose the name Engelbert Knoll Hinterfürnberg for his character because it rhymed with Nuremberg.

Postcards and Scrapbooks

The increasing demand for souvenirs and postcards during the rallies was a valuable source of income for the NSDAP. Heinrich Hoffmann's company was the official supplier and while it sold black and white cards during the early rallies, fourteen colour cards of Nuremberg's main attractions appeared later.

Hoffmann's company could not keep up with the demand and Nuremberg postcard producers including Ludwig Harren, the Intra Publishing House, Stoja Publishing House, F. Wilmy Printers and Zerreis Company & Co produced many more designs. Sets showed the Rally Grounds, parades and life on the Langwasser camp.

These companies also produced crude coloured cards by hand colouring black and white images and then mass producing them. The black SS and brown SA uniforms contrasted well with the red swastikas and white buildings. A colour quartet series of Nuremberg

Stores sold everything from uniforms to badges, postcards and posters.

Castle, the march through the Hauptmarket, the Congress Hall and the Zeppelin Field proved to be popular.

Hoffmann produced a cigarette card-style scrapbook called 'Germany Awakes; The Will, Struggle and Victory of the NSDAP' in 1933. While the flyleaf was decorated with photographs, buyers were encouraged to collect black and white or coloured cards to stick inside. Some of the proceeds were donated to the 'Reich Winter Help Fund' (*Winterhilfe*), the state run charity that collected money for the poor.

THE OFFICIAL PHOTOGRAPHER

Heinrich Hoffmann (1885–1957) was a Regensburg man who worked for several photographers before joining his father's Munich photograph studio in 1906. He opened his own studio in Munich in 1909 and in 1913 established Hoffmann Photo Report, specialising in press photographs, portraits and postcards. He served with the German air force in the First World War and following the Armistice he returned to press photography in Munich.

Hoffmann joined the People's Resistance (*Einwohnerwehr*) in 1919 and after meeting Dietrich Eckart – publisher of the NSDAP's newspaper the *People's Observer* (*Völkischer Beobachter*) – he became the Party's portrait photographer. He also became Hitler's personal photographer and following the November 1923 Putsch he published portraits of Hitler and a picture book called 'Germany Awakes in Pictures and Words'.

An unusual photograph of Hitler alone, speaking to the crowds.

By 1926 Hoffmann was working for the *People's Illustrated* (*Illustrierter Beobachter*), the NSDAP's weekly picture newspaper, and in 1929 he represented the NSDAP on Munich city council. At the same time a teenage Eva Braun began working for Hoffmann and Hitler met her in his photography studio. She would later become the Führer's constant companion (the pair married just before they committed suicide in the Berlin bunker on 30 April 1945).

Hoffman resigned from Munich town council in 1933 to concentrate on his photography and over the next six years took thousands of pictures of Nazi Party events. He published several picture books, including 'A People Honour its Führer' and 'The Olympic Games 1936', and they made him a fortune. He also proposed using Hitler's image on Germany's stamps and the income made a lot of money for them both.

Hoffmann was made responsible for confiscating degenerate art across Germany and then organised selling it abroad to raise foreign currency. He also selected exhibits for the German Art Exhibition in the Munich House of Art and was appointed professor when the exhibition opened in July 1938.

Hoffman joined the Reichstag in January 1940 and the following summer he organised the removal of pieces of art from French, Belgian and Dutch galleries. He was arrested by the US Army in April 1945 and his photograph collections were used as evidence in the Nuremberg war crimes trials. A large number are held by the National Archives and Records Administration (NARA) in Maryland, USA. He was found guilty in January 1946, imprisoned for four years, his professorial title was removed and his fortune was confiscated. He was released in 1950 and died in 1957 a poor man.

THE ARTISTIC PHOTOGRAPHER

Luise Aufsberg (1907–1976), nickname Lala, came from Immenstadt near the Swiss border and while she learned her skills in an Oberstdorf photograph shop, she honed them after 1931 with the Seitz and Porst photography company in Nuremberg. She also joined Nuremberg's photograph club and witnessed the growth of the Reich Party rallies.

Aufsberg first photographed the Party Rally in September 1937 and passed an advanced photography examination at the Weimar School for Handicraft and Applied Art in time for the 1938 rally. Her work contrasted with Hoffman's in that

Luise Aufsberg.

Aufsberg concentrated on fully realised, artistically presented images.

she focused on taking artistic photographs, concentrating on capturing moods rather than the pomp and ceremony of the parades and crowds. While her photographs were stylish, they were unfashionable with the Nazis and her work was not a success.

Aufsberg then returned to her home town and opened her own photo studio. She had her first major orders around 1941 and by the end of her career she had photographs in over 500 art books. Her archive of over 100,000 photographs and 45,000 negatives, many of them of southern Europe, were acquired by the Philipp University of Marburg.

THE OFFICIAL PAINTER

Ernst Vollbehr (1876–1960) was a Kiel man who studied painting in academies across Europe before travelling widely across South America and Africa, painting along the way. He produced over 1200 paintings and water colours during the First World War and while he covered many subjects, he ignored the horrors of the trenches. Between the wars he resumed his travels around the world and began painting industrial scenes to make money.

Vollbehr joined the NSDAP in July 1933 and painted scenes of the Reich Party Congress, the Olympic Games and autobahn projects. He was able to paint landscapes quickly and his works were the only ones published in the official picture books. He also published several of his own books.

Ernst Vollbehr paints a camouflaged bunker.

10

POLITICIANS AND POLICE CHIEFS

Five men would alter the course of history for Nuremberg after 1927, when the city became forever linked with the Nazi Party rallies. While the city's democratically elected Mayor, Hermann Luppe, opposed the NSDAP politicians for years, he was forced to resign when the Nazis seized power in 1933. His replacement, Willy Liebel, saw to it that the rally organisers had all the support they needed.

Franconia's Gauleiter, Julius Streicher, and his deputy Karl Holz, saw to it that Nazi plans were implemented and then enforced in and around the Nuremberg area. Nuremberg's Police Chief, Benno Martin, made sure the rallies received the full support of the city police force. He would later become head of both the SS and the Gestapo in the Nuremberg area.

NUREMBERG'S DEMOCRATIC MAYOR

Hermann Luppe (1874–1945) was a Kiel man who was awarded a doctorate in political sciences in 1896. He joined the German Democratic Party, was voted onto Frankfurt city council and was appointed deputy mayor in 1913. Following the Armistice, Luppe moved to Nuremberg, a Social Democratic-Liberal stronghold where the German Democratic Party only had eleven seats. Germany was facing troubled times and the people of Nuremberg were suffering when Otto Gessler stepped down as their mayor in March 1920. Luppe put his name forward and was elected Nuremberg's new mayor; he had been the only candidate. A coalition between the German Democratic Party and the Social Democrats wrested control from the minority Catholic Bavarian People's Party and their leader, Deputy Mayor Martin Treu, worked alongside Luppe on behalf of the people of Nuremberg.

Julius Streicher had recently joined the NSDAP and in May 1923 his supporters planned to take over the May Day celebrations. When Luppe took control of the city police to prevent the disturbances, the Bavarian government disapproved of his actions and brought the city police force under state control. They also appointed new police chief Heinrich Gareis, an opponent of Luppe's coalition and NSDAP supporter.

Mayor Hermann Luppe.

Under Gareis's control the police influenced local politics by allowing some rallies to go ahead and banning others. With the Nuremberg police favouring the National Socialists, Nuremberg was considered for the Party's second rally in August 1923 on Julius Streicher's recommendation. The previous one had been held in Munich but Nuremberg, with its central location, good rail connections and a large parade area offered better opportunities.

Streicher was right, 80,000 NSDAP supporters paraded through the streets, four times the number who attended the first rally. They then gathered in Luitpold Grove for a memorial service honouring the fallen of the First World War and those who had died fighting for the Party. Hitler also appeared four times in Luitpold Hall, speaking to 2000 members each time. Three months later Streicher and Hitler took part in the Munich Putsch and Hitler was arrested. The NSDAP was banned as an organisation and it would be banned from organising another rally in Nuremberg until 1927.

Meanwhile, the German Democratic Party was losing favour and although it only had three seats in 1924, Luppe was a proving to be a popular mayor. He worked tirelessly to improve conditions in the city, opening a new women's hospital and a municipal health office; the first in Bavaria. Under Luppe's guidance, the city council approved several housing programs and apartment blocks, improving living conditions for many working class families. He was also an advocate of vocational training and pumped funding into education. The city council promoted Franconia's culture through the Germanic National Museum, drama and opera. It provided new amenities including a public observatory and a planetarium. The airport was extended and upgraded, one of several improvements to the city's transport links.

One important contribution to Nuremberg under Luppe's stewardship was the building of a new recreation area in the south-east suburbs. During the mid 1920s a track-and-field stadium, complete with a football field and open-air swimming pool, was opened in the woods south of Dutzendteich Lakes. Their modern designs and landscaped surroundings were hailed as architectural triumphs. Little did Luppe know that the area would be used by his political opponents to stage their annual political rallies.

Despite the good work, members of Luppe's administration were constantly subjected to slander. Julius Streicher's newspaper *Der Stürmer* (see below) revelled in publishing outrageous stories about the Mayor and his associates. It was the start of a ten-year smear campaign of offensive newspaper stories and public insults and Luppe and Streicher faced each other in court on several occasions.

The Wall Street Crash in October 1929 and the subsequent collapse of the Germany economy resulted in electoral success for the extreme political parties, reducing the German Democratic Party to only two seats. Even so, Luppe continued as Mayor, facing many violent arguments with the newly elected NSDAP and Communist councillors in Nuremberg's council chambers.

The appointment of Hitler as Chancellor on 30 January 1933 and the Reichstag fire at the end of February changed everything. The implementation of the Enabling Act a few days later meant that the Nazis could do exactly what they wanted in local government. Nuremberg City Council was dissolved on 9 March 1933 and three days later Hermann Luppe was forced to resign after thirteen difficult years as Mayor; he was replaced by his nemesis, convicted Nazi Willy Liebel.

On 18 March Luppe was arrested and forced to submit his retirement; he was also dismissed from all other public positions. He was released on 23 April 1933 and expelled from the city and although he moved to Berlin the Nazis sought revenge and tried to cancel his pension through the courts. It was the price Luppe had to pay for reducing the NSDAP's influence on the Nuremberg council for so long.

Hermann Luppe eventually returned to his home city of Kiel. He was killed during an Allied air raid on 4 April 1945.

NUREMBERG'S NAZI MAYOR

Willy Liebel (1897–1945) came from Nuremberg and trained in his father's printing firm before and after serving in the trenches in the First World War. He became interested in politics and joined Erich Ludendorff's Tannenberg League (*Tannenbergbund*) and then the Reich Flag Party (*Reichsflagge*) before forming his own Old Reich Flag Party (*Altreichsflagge*). In November 1925 Liebel joined the NSDAP and was elected onto the city council in 1929; he was head of the NSDAP councillors in 1930. He was also an energetic member of the city's SA, rising to the rank of Obergruppenführer.

Following the implementation of the Enabling Act in March 1933, the Commissioner of the Bavarian Ministry of the Interior ordered Liebel to replace Luppe. Luppe was forced to resign and then arrested; on 27 April 1933 Liebel was confirmed as Nuremberg's mayor.

Mayor Willy Liebel stands to the right of Rudolf Hess.

Hitler, Speer and Liebel study the model of the Congress Hall.

Liebel was also appointed chairman of the Reich Party Congress Special Purpose Committee, coordinating the city's resources with organisations working on the Rally Grounds. Every summer he headed the city's committee, working closely with the rally organisers.

Although Liebel had a good working relationship with Police Chief Benno Martin, he had to fight off Gauleiter Streicher's repeated attempts to take control of the city. After Streicher was forced to stand down in February 1940 Liebel had to deal with his deputy, the equally power-crazed Karl Holz, during anti-Semitic actions across the city and the deportations of the Jews to the extermination camps.

Speer appointed Liebel head of the Ministry of Armaments Central Office in 1942 and two years later he was appointed head of the groups organising the reconstruction of Germany's bomb-damaged cities. Despite spending most of his time in Berlin, Liebel was still Nuremberg's mayor; if only in name.

Liebel returned to Nuremberg as the American troops closed in on the city and was immediately taken prisoner by diehard NSDAP members on 20 April. Some believe he was hoping to negotiate the city's surrender. Five days later his body was discovered but no one could decide if he had been executed or if he committed suicide.

FRANCONIA'S GAULEITER

Julius Streicher (1885–1946) was born in Fleinhausen, Bavaria, and after working as an elementary school teacher he joined the German Democratic Party in 1909. He joined the Army in 1914, serving in the trenches until the end of the war where he was awarded the Iron Cross for bravery.

Streicher was unhappy with Germany's post-war abject situation and he joined a number of political parties, including the German Nationalist Protection and Defence Federation (*Deutschvölkischer Schutz und Trutzbund*), the German Socialist Party (*Deutschsozialistische Partei*) and the German Working Community (*Deutsche Werkgemeinschaft*). After hearing Hitler speak in Munich he joined the NSDAP, encouraging his friends and supporters to do the same. The transfer doubled the NSDAP's membership and brought Nazi politics to Nuremberg.

In May 1923 Streicher founded a newspaper, *Der Stürmer* (The Stormer or The Attacker), a fiercely anti-Semitic propaganda broadsheet which revelled in slander rather than report-ing facts. He marched alongside Hitler in the unsuccessful November Munich Putsch and was lucky to escape imprisonment. Streicher was appointed Gauleiter of the Franconia region when the Party re-organised in 1925 and was also elected to the Bavarian Landtag.

Streicher's attempts to discredit his opponents were merciless and he stuck to his unof-ficial motto of 'something always sticks', repeatedly printing slanderous reports in his newspaper, ignoring the threat of lawsuits. Most of his attacks targeted politicians and Jewish businessmen but anyone who got in the way of his political ambitions was consid-ered fair game.

The appointment of Hitler as Chancellor in January 1933 heralded a new start in German politics and by April 1933 the NSDAP's Gauleiters had enormous power. The Franconia area included Nuremberg and Streicher immediately organised a one-day boy-

Julius Streicher, Franconia's Gauleiter.

cott of Jewish businesses. He soon became a despotic leader, attracting nicknames such as the Beast of Franconia, the King of Nuremberg and the *Frankenführer*; he also revelled in the title 'Jew-Baiter Number One'. He was constantly at loggerheads with Nuremberg's mayor, Willy Liebel, as the two fought for control over the city.

The circulation of *Der Stürmer* continued to increase, peaking at 480,000 in 1935, and Hitler made it clear that it was his favourite newspaper. Streicher's publishing firm also released three anti-Semitic books for children, which were introduced into the school curriculum.

In the summer of 1938 Streicher went as far as ordering an attack on the Nuremberg Synagogue, a foretaste of what would happen when Nazi leaders ordered attacks on synagogues across Germany in November. The attacks would be collectively known as the Night of Broken Glass, or *Kristallnacht*.

Streicher's excessive behaviour was frowned upon by many senior Party officials and it soon became clear that he had personally profited from the seizure of Jewish properties. While the Party was able to buy them for a fraction of their true value, individuals

Streicher strikes a confident, Mussolini-like pose as he speaks to the crowds.

were not allowed to profit. Streicher was also making slanderous comments against senior Party officials, in particular Hermann Göring. His increasingly eccentric behaviour was an embarrassment and in February 1940 he was stripped of all Party offices, sacked as Gauleiter and forced to withdraw from the public eye.

Streicher survived until the end of the war and was captured by US troops on 23 May 1945 in the town of Waidring, Austria. At the Nuremberg trials he was found guilty of crimes against humanity for inciting anti-Semitic behaviour; he was executed.

FRANCONIA'S DEPUTY GAULEITER

Karl Holz (1895–1945) was a Nuremberg man who was wounded several times in the trenches in the First World War. In 1920 he joined Julius Streicher's German Socialist Party (*Deutsch Sozialistische Partei*) and followed his friend when he transferred to the NSDAP two years later.

Although Holz was elected onto Nuremberg City Council in 1924, he resigned the following year to concentrate on his work in the SA, rising to the rank of Gruppenführer. He also joined Streicher's team at *Der Stürmer* and was appointed editor-in-chief in 1927.

Holz's fortunes improved when the Nazis seized power in 1933 and he left the newspaper team to work as a ministerial adviser. His loyalty to Streicher was rewarded in January 1934 when he was appointed Franconia's Deputy Gauleiter. Seven months later he became the *Kreisleiter*, or Party organiser, for Nuremberg city, and in November the SA promoted him to Brigadeführer.

Streicher and Holz ruled Nuremberg with a rod of iron for the next six years, making sure that Nazi policies were pursued vigorously across the city. They were particularly energetic in their efforts to strip members of the Jewish community of their assets; in fact too energetic. In 1940 Holz was temporarily stripped of his offices pending investigations into misappropriation of Jewish assets.

Streicher lines up with the Party leaders; he was at odds with many of them.

Holz was acquitted and was appointed Reich Defence Commissar of Franconia in November 1942. He was also was appointed temporary Gauleiter of Franconia in March 1943 and the appointment was made permanent following Streicher's dismissal in November 1944. During this period he presided over the deportation of Nuremberg's Jews to extermination camps in Poland.

Holz's reign of terror came to an end on 18 April 1945 as troops of the 3rd US Infantry Division advanced though Nuremberg's ruined streets. He barricaded himself in the City Police Headquarters along with Mayor Willy Liebel and other officials. It is believed he may have shot Liebel when he suggested negotiating the surrender the city to the American troops. Holz died two days later but whether he died in battle or chose to take his own life is not known.

NUREMBERG'S CHIEF OF POLICE

Benno Martin (1893–1975) came from Kaiserslautern and after serving in the First World War he joined the Freikorps. He attended university and gained a law doctorate before joining the Nuremberg police department in 1923. Over the next ten years he rose

Martin's police force made sure that no one interfered with the NSDAP parades.

through the ranks until he became the city's Chief of Police. Martin was a key player behind the selection of Nuremberg after the ban on NSDAP Party rallies was lifted in 1927. Julius Streicher made it clear that the city police force would cooperate with the NSDAP and prevent interference from rival political parties.

Martin joined the NSDAP in 1933 and the SS in 1934, becoming Nuremberg's police chief, the city SS leader and area Gestapo chief all at the same time. In this powerful role he played an important part in making sure that the city police accommodated the rallies He also acquired the nickname 'The Black Knight' and was known as 'Himmler's Man in Nuremberg'.

Martin made sure that the police and the Gestapo worked together to arrest 'enemies of the State' and to force Jews out of the city. Once the Holocaust was underway he played a key role in organising the deportation of Franconian Jews to Auschwitz; he was acquitted of charges after the war.

11

ANTI-SEMITISM AT NUREMBERG

One of the cornerstones of early NSDAP politics was to blame the Jewish community for many or all of Germany's problems, be it the economy, unemployment or losing the First World War. Once in power the Nazis were able to turn their ideas into policies and it was not long before the first anti-Jewish actions. The deadly combination of Gauleiter Streicher's pro-active anti-Semitic stance and Police Chief Martin's pro-Nazi attitude meant that assaults on Nuremberg's Jewish community were worse than in many other German cities.

The city's SA participated in the first national boycott of Jewish businesses on 1 April 1933, stopping customers from entering shops and stores. On 20 July SA storm troopers were given orders to raid the houses of 400 affluent Jewish families across the city, with instructions to confiscate cash and savings accounts. Around 300 male Jews were arrested, taken to wasteland and beaten up. The police did nothing.

The continuing threat of SA violence and the lack of police support for the Jewish community meant that many families left Nuremberg, either hoping to emigrate or live with friends in the country where they less likely to be targeted. By March 1934 the number of Jews in the city had fallen below 1500 and the exodus continued; by 1937 only a couple of hundred were left. On 8 November 1937 an exhibition called the 'The Eternal Jew' opened in the city and thousands of visitors came to see the anti-Semitic displays connecting Judaism and Bolshevism.

Those who remained behind were subjected to the many pogroms enforced by the Nazi State. Gauleiter Streicher's staff and city officials worked together to acquire Jewish properties, through threats and force. They were bought for a fraction of their value but when an inquiry uncovered corruption, it denounced the sales and advised punishment. In 1940 both Streicher and his deputy Holz were suspended when investigations were completed; Holz would eventually replace Streicher.

The pogroms restricted freedom of movement, employment, education and the holding of financial assets. The increasing restrictions excluded the tiny Jewish community from society, forcing them to rely on friends and family for employment and essentials.

After prolonged discussions, during which the Jewish community refused to sell the main Synagogue (*Hauptsynagoge*), the city council expropriated the building on 3 August

SA troops put up anti-Semitic posters.

1938. A week later Streicher ordered the destruction of the Great Synagogue and the adjacent community building because he believed they were 'spoiling the look of the city'. The smashing of windows and demolition of the walls and roof was a preview of what was being planned for the rest of Germany. The murder of the German diplomat Ernst vom Rath in the Paris Embassy by the young Polish Jew Herschel Grynszpan was the catalyst the Nazis had been looking for. During the early hours of 10 November Reinhard Heydrich, combined head of the Gestapo, the Criminal Police and the Party Secret Police, issued instructions to the State Police and the SA to attack Jewish communities.

In Nuremberg hundreds of SA men assembled in the main square in the early hours before marching off to set fire to the Orthodox Adas Israel synagogue behind the hotel where Hitler stayed during the rallies. Others did the same to the Ahiezer prayer hall; the police and fire brigades did nothing to stop them.

The SA then went on the rampage against the Jewish community, ransacking apartments, smashing up businesses and attacking people. 160 Jews were arrested and beaten up in the city's prison before they were carted off to Dachau concentration camp for a short time. At least sixteen were beaten to death, ten committed suicide and many others were injured. The remaining Jews left the city after the violence of Kristallnacht.

Clearing up broken glass after a night of violence.

NUREMBERG'S ANTI-SEMITIC NEWSPAPER

The first issue of the *Der Stürmer* appeared in Nuremberg on 20 April 1923 and it soon became a popular weekly tabloid newspaper across Germany. As previously mentioned, the editor was Franconia's Gauleiter, Julius Streicher, and he delighted in running obscene and tasteless articles. He also published slanderous articles against NSDAP opponents, resulting in court cases and breaks in publication. The newspaper also published letters from senior Nazi officials, letters which could have dragged the official party paper, *Völkischer Beobachter* (People's Observer), into the courts.

In 1927 it only had a circulation of 27,000 and many copies were put in road-side display cases so anyone could read them, particularly the unemployed who had no money for such luxuries. Its popularity increased at the same rate as the NSDAP membership and by 1935 the circulation was 480,000 and it made Streicher a rich man.

Der Stürmer

Deutsches Wochenblatt zum Kampfe um die Wahrheit

HERAUSGEBER: JULIUS STREICHER

| Nummer 19 | Nürnberg, im Mai 1937 | 15. Jahr 1937 |

Jüdische Blutschande

Der Prozeß Weil in Frankenthal (Saarpfalz) / Ein Jude schändet sein nichtjüdisches Stiefkind

Schauerliche Verbrechen eines echten Talmudjuden / Schützt die deutsche Jugend!

Schach dem Teufel

Gesetz allein schützt unsere Jugend nicht / Dem Juden ist Gebot, daß er es bricht /
Des Juden Treiben könnt ihr nur beenden / Versteht ihr das Gesetz scharf anzuwenden

Aus dem Inhalt

Rassenschande auch in Rumänien
Brief eines Japaners
Berliner Brief:
   Die Berliner „Scala" / Das Gastspiel
   Aushnn / Ein Jude verspottet Mussolini
   Devisen in Lederknöpfen

Die Juden sind unser Unglück!

A typical front page of *Der Stürmer*.

All the while, *Der Stürmer* poured bile on the Jewish community with three types of anti-Semitic articles. Firstly, making accusations about sexual crimes; secondly, making slanderous claims about Jewish businesses; and finally, making outrageous claims about activities in the Jewish community. The newspaper often published anti-Semitic caricatures with exaggerated facial features and misshapen bodies. Streicher specialised in searching for medieval stories, looking to revive myths about ancient Jewish religious practices including child sacrifice.

It was said that *Der Stürmer* was Hitler's favourite newspaper, and he read each issue from front to back. While Himmler also supported it, Göring hated it and Schirach banned it from Hitler Youth hostels. Despite Streicher's fall from grace with senior Nazis, he continued to publish the newspaper until the end of the war and between August 1941 and September 1944 he published articles demanding the extermination of the Jewish race.

Streicher was tried at Nuremberg and charged with being an accessory to murder by inciting Germans to exterminate Jews in the pages of *Der Stürmer*. He was found guilty and hanged in October 1946.

THE NUREMBERG LAWS

Nuremberg was connected with the Nazi anti-Semitic actions through a series of laws announced at the 1935 rally. Demands for laws banning marriage and sexual relations

Göring (on the right) proposed the Nuremberg Laws.

between and Aryans and non-Aryans were ignored by the Nazi hierarchy to begin with. However, the Ministry of the Interior spent the next two and a half years arguing over the definition of a Jew. Perverse as it sounds, the Nazi regime wanted a legal foundation to anti-Semitic actions sponsored by the government.

Many long-serving Nazis (known as the Old Guard or *Alte Kämpfer*) were frustrated by the lack of action and they continued to organise random attacks against Jewish communities. While a Gestapo report in the spring of 1935 confirmed the Party dissent against the lack of anti-Semitic laws, the public were increasingly outraged by the sporadic outbreaks of violence. On 8 August the NSDAP stopped the attacks, concerned about a public backlash.

Ministers discussed the economic effects of attacks against Jewish communities on 20 August 1935, with a view to introducing anti-Semitic laws to appease both the Old Guard and the public. While Dr Hjalmar Schacht, Economics Minister and Reichsbank President, believed that arbitrary attacks were harmful to the economy, the NSDAP representative, Adolf Wagner, wanted the Jews economically excluded. Wagner won the argument and everyone left the meeting, looking forward to the imminent Nuremberg Rally.

Police harassment in the Jewish community.

The rally opened on 10 September and for the first time since 1543 the Reichstag parliament met in the city. Hitler's plans to speak about the Italian actions against Ethiopia were quashed when Foreign Minister Konstantin von Neurath pointed out they would contradict his calls for peace. While the Führer considered how to address the senior foreign diplomats invited to the Reichstag meeting, senior NSDAP physician Gerhard Wagner announced that a law preventing marriages between Aryans and Jews was imminent. An immediate decision was taken to introduce new laws and Dr Wilhelm Stuckart, the State Secretary of the Interior ordered Dr Bernhard Lösener and Franz Medicus to fly to Nuremberg.

They arrived on 14 September and only had 24 hours to draft the two new laws, writing them up on menu cards, the only available writing paper. The following day Hitler announced them both in front of the Reichstag; Reichstag President, Hermann Göring, proposed them and they were accepted. 'The Reich Citizenship Law' and 'The Law for the Protection of German Blood and German Honour' collectively became known as the Nuremberg Laws.

The Reich Citizenship Law determined who was a citizen of the Reich and who was not, dividing the population into two groups which could be treated differently under the law. It effectively stripped Jews of their German citizenship. While citizens of pure German blood were known as Reich Citizens, subjects of the state were known as Nationals. The main articles of the law are given below:

Article 1.1   A subject of the State is a person who belongs to the protective union of the German Reich, and who therefore has particular obligations towards the Reich.

Article 1.2   The status of subject is acquired in accordance with the provisions of the Reich and State Law of Citizenship.

Article 2.1   A citizen of the Reich is that subject only who is of German or kindred blood and who, through his conduct, shows that he is both desirous and fit to serve the German people and Reich faithfully.

Article 2.2   The right to citizenship is acquired by the granting of Reich citizenship papers.

Article 2.3   Only the citizen of the Reich enjoys full political rights in accordance with the provision of the laws.

The Reich citizenship papers were never introduced.

The Law for the Protection of German Blood and German Honour was split into three parts and the important sections are listed below. Breaches of the law were punishable with a fine, hard labour, or imprisonment: The first part prevented citizens and Jews from marrying or having sexual relationships and it immediately came into effect.

J# 9863/ 5012

Gesetz zum Schutze des deutschen Blutes und der deutschen Ehre.

Vom 15.September 1935.

Durchdrungen von der Erkenntnis, daß die Reinheit des deutschen Blutes die Voraussetzung für den Fortbestand des Deutschen Volkes ist, und beseelt von dem unbeugsamen Willen, die Deutsche Nation für alle Zukunft zu sichern, hat der Reichstag einstimmig das folgende Gesetz beschlossen, das hiermit verkündet wird:

§ 1

(1) Eheschließungen zwischen Juden und Staatsangehörigen deutschen oder artverwandten Blutes sind verboten. Trotzdem geschlossene Ehen sind nichtig, auch wenn sie zur Umgehung dieses Gesetzes im Ausland geschlossen sind.

(2) Die Nichtigkeitsklage kann nur der Staatsanwalt erheben.

§ 2

Außerehelicher Geschlechtsverkehr zwischen Juden und Staatsangehörigen deutschen oder artverwandten Blutes ist verboten.

§ 3

Juden dürfen weibliche Staatsangehörige deutschen oder artverwandten Blutes unter 45 Jahren in ihrem Haushalt nicht beschäftigen.

§ 4

(1) Juden ist das Hissen der Reichs- und Nationalflagge und das Zeigen der Reichsfarben verboten.

(2) Dagegen ist ihnen das Zeigen der jüdischen Farben gestattet. Die Ausübung dieser Befugnis steht unter staatlichem Schutz.

.∕.

The first page of the Nuremberg Laws.

Section 1.1   Marriages between Jews and citizens of German or kindred blood are forbidden. Marriages concluded in defiance of this law are void, even if, for the purpose of evading this law, they were concluded abroad.

Section 2   Sexual relations outside marriage between Jews and nationals of German or kindred blood are forbidden.

The 35,000 mixed race marriages between Germans and Jews were known as Blood Dishonours and they would be annulled by the Public Prosecutor. The couples would soon be pressurised into getting a divorce by the authorities. Further cohabitation between German Aryans and Jews would be classified as a criminal activity called Race Defilement and perpetrators were denounced in the press. After July 1938 the Marriage Law allowed couples to have their marriages annulled on racial grounds; unsurprisingly, it placed a huge strain on many marriages.

The second part of the law banned Jews from employing Germans as domestic servants and it came into effect on the 1 January 1936.

Section 3   Jews will not be permitted to employ female citizens of German or kindred blood as domestic servants.

This was included in response to lurid claims about male Jewish employers having sexual fantasies about their female German servants.

The third part of the law referred to displaying flags on houses and businesses and it came into immediate effect.

Section 4.1   Jews are forbidden to display the Reich and national flag or the national colours.

Section 4.1   Jews are permitted to display the Jewish colours.

Section four worked alongside another law announced on the sixth day of the Rally, the Reich Flag Law. The law was drafted in response to an incident in New York on 26 July 1935 when anti-Nazi demonstrators had taken the swastika flag from SS *Bremen* and thrown it into the Hudson River. Although the German Consul had protested, the United States government refused to take action because it was the flag of a political party and was not Germany's national flag. The Reich Flag Law meant that the swastika could not be discredited again. The second part of the law made it an offence not to display the national flag on national holidays because flags were going to be used to divide the population visibly.

The Reich Citizenship Law did pose the question: who was a Jew? On 1 November 1935 the question of the 200,000 individuals of mixed race, or *Mischlinge*, was answered by Dr Bernhard Lösener of the Ministry of the Interior. Anyone with three or four Jewish grandparents was a Jew. Anyone with two Jewish grandparents was a First Degree Half-Jew; they were Jewish if they had married another Jew or if they practised the Jewish

§ 5

(1) Wer dem Verbot des § 1 zuwiderhandelt, wird mit Zuchthaus bestraft.

(2) Der Mann, der dem Verbot des § 2 zuwiderhandelt, wird mit Gefängnis oder mit Zuchthaus bestraft.

(3) Wer den Bestimmungen der §§ 3 oder 4 zuwiderhandelt, wird mit Gefängnis bis zu einem Jahr und mit Geldstrafe oder mit einer dieser Strafen bestraft.

§ 6

Der Reichsminister des Innern erläßt im Einvernehmen mit dem Stellvertreter des Führers und dem Reichsminister der Justiz die zur Durchführung und Ergänzung des Gesetzes erforderlichen Rechts- und Verwaltungsvorschriften.

§ 7

Das Gesetz tritt am Tage nach der Verkündung, § 3 jedoch erst am 1.Januar 1936 in Kraft.

Nürnberg, den 15.September 1935,
am Reichsparteitag der Freiheit.

Der Führer und Reichskanzler.

Der Reichsminister des Innern.

Der Reichsminister der Justiz.

Dr. Gürtner

Der Stellvertreter des Führers.

The second page of the Nuremberg Laws.

religion. They could also be treated as a Jew when it suited the authorities. Anyone with only one Jewish grandparent was a Second Degree Quarter-Jew and they were considered to be Reich Citizens when it suited the authorities. Relationships with Jews were also discouraged by classifying any babies born out of wedlock as Jews.

THE NUREMBERG BOMB PLOT

Opposition to the Third Reich was limited owing to the strenuous efforts the Nazi regime made to suppress enemies of the State. The Police, Gestapo and SS intelligence service worked separately and together to identify, arrest and interrogate suspects. Those suspected of terrorist activities were imprisoned in a concentration camp while the guilty would be executed.

One planned attack involving Helmut Hirsch (1916–1937) was directed against Nuremberg and although the target is not known, it was believed to be either the Nazi Party headquarters or the newspaper plant producing the anti-Semitic propaganda newspaper *Der Stürmer*.

Hirsch was from Stuttgart and as a teenager he joined the youth movement called the 'German Boys' (*Deutsche Jungenschaft*). The announcement of the Nuremberg Laws in September 1935 meant that as a Jew, he was excluded from German universities; the Jungenschaft was also outlawed around the same time.

Desperate to continue his education, Hirsch left Germany for Prague, Czechoslovakia, and enrolled in the architecture school of the German Institute of Technology. He also became involved with the Black Front, a group of anti-Hitler German exiles led by Otto Strasser.

Although Hirsch's family arrived in Prague in 1936, they knew nothing of his undercover motives when he left for Germany in December, unaware that German agents were following him. He was supposed to meet Heinrich Grunov, working under the alias Dr Beer, who would give him two suitcases containing explosives. However, Hirsch suffered last-minute nerves and headed to Stuttgart to talk the bomb plot over with a friend. He checked into a hotel when the friend failed to turn up and was promptly arrested by the Gestapo.

Hirsch was interrogated in Stuttgart and then taken to Berlin's infamous Plötzensee Prison where he was charged with conspiracy to commit high treason. He was also charged with criminal intent and possession of explosives, even though he had none when he was arrested. After nine weeks in solitary confinement Hirsch appeared in court where it became clear he had been betrayed by an informer in the Black Front. He did not deny his involvement in the bomb plot and when asked if he wanted to assassinate Hitler, he replied yes, and the international press reported that was his plan.

Hirsch was found guilty and condemned to death and when the news was announced there were calls for clemency from the International Red Cross, the Society of Friends, and an international association of lawyers. The United States reinstated the lapsed citizenship of Hirsch's father and on 22 April 1937 Hirsch was declared an American citizen although he had never been to America. Appeals by William E. Dodd, the American ambassador in Berlin, fell on deaf ears and on 4 June 1937 Hirsch was executed.

12

NUREMBERG TODAY

The Rally Grounds are located around Dutzendteich Lakes, two miles south east of Nuremberg's old town. People had been visiting the area since the turn of the century, either relaxing in the parks, walking round the lakes or visit the zoo and sports arenas. After 1933 they came to the venue for the annual Reich Party Rally where structures were improved and added until the Rally Grounds covered 11km².

The Nazis converted existing structures until Albert Speer was commissioned to redesign the Rally Grounds in April 1934. He planned to add halls, parade grounds and exhibition centres and anticipated a completion date of August 1945. Using huge amounts of labour, including slave labour, work progressed at a tremendous rate but as we have seen the 1939 rally was cancelled when Germany invaded Poland. Interest in the Rally Grounds declined, and work ground to a halt as the tide of war turned in the Allies' favour.

Towards the end of the war, Seventh US Army closed in on Nuremberg in April 1945 and 45th Division captured the Rally Grounds on the 18th. A few days later the first of many ceremonies were held on the Zeppelin Field to celebrate the liberation of the city and it was renamed Soldiers' Field, a place where American troops listened to jazz bands and played baseball.

Dutzendteich is once again a leisure area but many of the Nazi structures are still standing in various states of decay. It is possible to walk and drive around the Rally Grounds but it is advisable to start a tour with a visit to the Document Centre (*Dokumentationszentrum*) where films and photographs illustrate what happened here in the 1930s.

THE DOCUMENTATION CENTRE

A museum dedicated to the history of the Nuremberg Rally Grounds is situated in the north wing of the Congress Hall. There is a car park (a small fee is charged) next to the Congress Hall and the entrance is at the top of a flight of steps jutting out from the north-west corner of the building. The museum's address is:

The incomplete Congress Hall.

Faszination und Gewalt (Fascination and Terror)
Dokumentationszentrum Reichsparteitagsgelände
Bayernstraße 110, 90471 Nürnberg
Tel: (0911) 231-5666 Fax: (0911) 231-8410
Email: dokumentationszentrum@stadt.nuernberg.de

The museum is open from 9:00am until 6:00pm on weekdays and from 10:00am until 6:00pm on weekends. The admission fees in 2011 were €5.00 for adults, €2.50 for children with other reductions and special reduced rates for large parties and school groups. Although the exhibits are in German, audio language handsets are available.

   The top floor has a permanent exhibition and the visitor is guided through 19 aspects of the rise and fall of the National Socialist movement and the part the Nuremberg Rally Grounds played in it. The visit ends on an elevated walkway jutting out into the centre of the Congress Hall and visitors can see how the crumbling inner brick walls compare with the outer granite façade. The lower floor has areas for temporary exhibits, a café and a bookshop.

THE CONGRESS HALL (KONGRESSHALLE)

Work started on the building in 1935 and it was designed to seat 50,000 delegates under-cover. Ludwig Ruff planned the building along the lines of Rome's Coliseum but work

Inside the shell of the Congress Hall.

was abandoned in 1943 before the interior seating area and roof had been started. It is now home to the Document Centre and the Nuremberg Symphony Orchestra while other areas are used for storage.

Two obelisks were going to stand astride the Great Road outside the Congress Hall and an exhibition centre was planned to the west. An archway was also supposed to straddle the Great Road. They were never built and the area is now a car park used by Nuremberg's biannual fairground. The Nuremberg Zoo occupied the area beyond the car park until the Nazis closed it; the Culture Hall planned for the site did not get off the drawing board.

LUITPOLD ARENA AND LUITPOLD HALL

Cross the main road, Bayern Straße, outside the Congress Hall and enter Luitpold Grove. The area staged the Bavarian Exhibition after 1906 and the park and hall were the venues for the first two Nazi rallies held in the city in 1927 and 1929. The War Memorial or Hall of Honour was built on the east side of the park in 1930 and it is a useful orientation point.

Luitpold Grove was turned into a parade ground for 150,000 and while the Tribune of Honour faced the Hall of Honour there were grandstands on the remaining three sides. The grandstands were removed after the war and the area was turned back into a park. The Hall of Honour is now dedicated to the victims of war.

Luitpold Grove's Hall of Honour.

Luitpold Hall stood at the south-west corner of Luitpold Arena and the glass and steel building was remodelled between 1933 and 1935 so it could be used for the Party Congress meetings. The building was badly damaged during Allied air raids and the ruins were removed after the war, only the steps remain.

Re-cross Bayern Straße either by the footbridge or at street level to visit the Great Road.

THE GREAT ROAD (GROSSESTRASSE)

The Great Road passes between the Dutzendteich Lakes, the twin lakes which were once surrounded by leisure areas and beer gardens. At 80 metres wide and over two kilometres long, the Road is impressive. It connects Luitpold Arena to the Mars Field and Speer designed the road to point towards Nuremberg Castle, symbolically linking the Nazi Rally Grounds with the city's Imperial heritage. Tall trees now obscure the view. Many of the original slabs at the north end have been restored and sections of the ruined steps built for the crowds can be seen along the east edge. The Great Road served as a landing strip for the American Air Force immediately after the city was captured; it is now used as an overflow parking area for the Trade Fair Centre.

The Great Road.

THE GREAT GERMAN STADIUM (*DEUTSCHE STADION*)

Speer planned to build a large stone podium half way down the east side of the Great Road where Hitler would salute the passing parades. The Great German Stadium was going to be built across the road (to the right, looking south) and the horseshoe-shaped structure was planned to hold 400,000 spectators. Although the foundation stone was dedicated on 9 September 1937 the excavations were half finished when work was abandoned in 1942.

The foundation stone was removed in 2001 and Silbersee, a lake formed by the excavations, and Silberbuck, a hill made of rubble from the bombed city, now occupy the site. Nürnberger Messe, the Nuremberg Trade Fair Centre, home of the annual Toy Fair, is just to the south.

Return to your car to visit the rest of the Rally Grounds. Turn right out of the Congress Hall car park onto Bayern Straße. Dutzendteich railway station, where the visitors to the Rally Grounds arrived, is above the railway bridge after 500 metres. Pass beneath the railway bridge and turn right at the traffic lights after 100 metres, heading south onto Regensburger Straße.

Hitler dedicates the foundation stone of the German Stadium on 9 September 1937.

THE ZEPPELIN ARENA AND GRANDSTAND

Heading south east, the area to the left (east) of the road was the site of the Strength through Joy Town, the area dedicated to German culture; the wooden halls were destroyed during the war.

Head south east for 700 metres. Note the Transformer Building (*Umspannwerk*) to the right just before the crossroads. The structure was built to power the searchlights used during the night-time parades. The building now houses a fast food restaurant but the chipped out eagle and swastika over the doorway can still be seen.

Turn right at the traffic lights and head under the railway bridge and follow Hans–Kalb Straße as it turns sharp right and then left. The Zeppelin Field is immediately in front. Park your car to visit the Transformer Building and the Zeppelin Grandstand.

The Zeppelin Field is still an arena and the ruins of the grandstand can be visited. On 22 April 1945 General Alexander Patch awarded five Medals of Honor to soldiers of 3rd Division in the arena and three days later the swastika on top of the grandstand was blown to pieces. The Hall of Pillars was demolished in 1967 because the columns were unstable while the upper parts of the structure were removed a few years later.

It is possible to climb the steps and stand on the speaker's podium where steps and a railing have been added. The arena is now used for leisure activities and Nuremberg city racetrack passes immediately in front of the grandstand. Round the back of the grandstand you can see the doors where party delegates entered the building; you can also see one of the huge bowls that was filled with burning oil.

Walk south west along Karl-Steigelmann Straße, following the embankment of the Zeppelin Field, passing the abutments where swastika flags once flew.

The Transformer House for the Zeppelin Field.

What remains of the Zeppelin Tribune.

The speaker's podium and the assembly hall of the Zeppelin Tribune

The buttresses around the perimeter of the Zeppelin Field.

The Franken Stadium and the Zeppelin Field.

THE FRANKEN STADIUM

The entrance to the Franken Stadium is after 400 metres. The stadium was opened in 1928 and used to stage the Hitler Youth Day from 1933 to 1938. The stadium became home to FC Nuremberg in 1966 and it underwent several refurbishments to bring it up to standard; it hosted five World Cup games in 2006.

THE MARS FIELD (MÄRZFELD)

Return to your car and head south east (with the *Zeppelintribüne* immediately behind you) along Beuthhener Straße. The road curves to the right and becomes Schönleben Straße as it crosses the Great Road to the right after 1500 metres. The site of the Mars Field (Märzfeld) was to the left of the road.

Speer designed the huge arena, for 160,000 spectators, to replace the Zeppelin Field. It would have been 600 metres along its longest side with 26 towers complete with Josef

Thorak's sculptures guarding the entrance. Only eleven towers had been completed when work stopped in 1943 and they were demolished by 1967 to make way for Langwasser apartment blocks. Large parts of the area have been built over and only a few crumbling pieces of the foundations remain in the bushes.

THE CAMPING GROUNDS

The Langwasser camp was built to the south of Märzfeld and it could accommodate 200,000 men. All that remains today is the water tower standing on a hill overlooking the old camping grounds. It is situated 100 metres south east of the junction of Breslauer Straße and Oelser Straße. A new railway station was built for the visitors between Märzfeld and the camps; only a few ruins are left.

SS BARRACKS

Continue past the Great Road and turn right at the traffic lights, heading north along Münchener Straße towards the centre of Nuremberg. Turn left at the set of traffic lights after two kilometres and then right at the first of traffic lights into Altersberger Straße.

The large building on the left was the SS barracks built between 1936 and 1939. It was the headquarters of the 2nd US Armored Cavalry Regiment and known as the Merrell

The façade of the old SS Barracks.

Barracks after the war. The building was returned to the German government in 1995 and is now used as a document centre.

Head north and drive under a tunnel after 1500 metres; the railway station is 200 metres west of the tunnel. Park your vehicle on the street here and walk back to the station to start your visit of Nuremberg's old town.

NUREMBERG CITY CENTRE

Hitler arrived in Nuremberg at the railway station (*Hauptbahnhof*) and made his way to his hotel. Head west along Frauentorgraben, passing the Nuremberg Opera House on the left after 400 metres; Deutscher Hof Hotel is the next building. He stayed in a large first-floor room and often reviewed troops from the window as they marched past. The building was extended in 1936 and the Führer's new room had a balcony. The balcony no longer exists but other parts of the building are still the same.

Nuremberg railway station.

The Deutscher Hof Hotel next to Nuremberg's Opera House.

Return to the railway station and cross the road at Königstor, one of the many medieval towers protecting the city wall. Turn left into Königstraße, to the right of the tower, heading into the city centre. The streets were decked with flags and filled with spectators during the rallies as the Nazi organisations gathered in this area ready to march past the Führer.

HAUPTMARKT

Continue north past St Lorenz's Church on the right and turn left (west) just before the Pegnitz River. After 100 metres turn right (north), crossing the river over Fleisch Bridge; Hauptmarkt is 100m beyond the river.

The square has served as a market place since the fourteenth century and it is the focal point of the famous Christmas Market. The fourteenth-century Church of Our Lady (*Frauenkirche*) is on the east side while the town hall (*Rathaus*) stands at the north-west corner; the original building was destroyed during the war. The focal point of the square

Troops marched over Fleisch Bridge, or Meat Bridge, to cross the Pegnitz River.

The Church of Our Lady (Frauenkirche) overlooks the Hauptmarkt.

Hitler's entourage stood by the Beautiful Fountain during the march past.

is the multi-tiered ornate Beautiful Fountain rising 20 metres into the air in front of the town hall. Hitler stood by the fountain, surrounded by his henchmen, as they reviewed the passing columns of marching troops heading up the hill towards the castle.

Hauptmarkt was renamed Adolf-Hitler-Platz in 1933 but the 3rd US Division called it Eiserner-Michael-Platz, or Iron Mike Square, in honour of their commanding officer, General John O'Daniel. American troops held a parade in the square on 20 April 1945 (Hitler's birthday), following the three-day fight for the city.

NUREMBERG CASTLE

Follow Burg Straße up the hill and enter Nuremberg Castle via Heaven's Gate. The opening hours are 9:00am to 17:00pm from April to September and 10:00am to 16:00pm from October to March.

Emperor Heinrich III built the Imperial Castle, or *Kaiserberg*, on the outcrop of rock overlooking the town. A new wall was built in the eleventh century to protect the Holy Roman Empire's Imperial Diets. Guardians looked after the castle and they built the adjacent Burgrave's Castle. There are fantastic views across the old city from the top of the

Troops marched past the town hall, up the hill to the castle.

Nuremberg Castle.

Sinwell Tower while the huge Emperor's Hall, Knight's Hall and Imperial Stables are just some of the buildings that are now home to various museums.

JULIUS STREICHER'S GAUHAUS

Retrace your steps to the Hauptmarkt, leaving the square at the south-east corner, and cross the river via Museumsbrücke. Follow Königstraße for 300 metres and then turn left into Lorenzer Straße alongside St Lorenz's Church. Pass beneath Mareintor Gate, one of the gates in the medieval city wall, and continue east along Marienstraße. The Gauhaus is after 300 metres on the north side (left hand side) of Marienplatz. The building was built in 1937 for the Franconia Gauleiter Julius Streicher. It was severely damaged during the battle for the city but was rebuilt in the original 1930s style after the war.

Head back along Marienstraße and take the first left into Gleißbühlstraße; the railway station is at the end of the street.

THE NUREMBERG TRIALS

Many of the speakers at the Nuremberg Rallies, including Herman Göring, Rudolf Hess, Julius Striecher, Robert Ley and Alfred Rosenberg, returned to the city in October 1945 to appear in the Nuremberg trials. They were held in the Nuremberg Palace of Justice and

Gauleiter Julius Streicher's headquarters.

Nuremberg's Courthouse where the Nazis were tried and some were then executed.

the building is 2km west of the railway station. Some may wish to make the 30-minute walk but the underground runs from the railway station close to the courthouse (four stops west to Bärenschanze station).

Alternatively drive to the courthouse following Frauentorgraben as it heads west alongside the old city walls. Continue past the Opera House and continue straight on at Am Plärrer square after half a mile (where the city wall turns north) onto Fürther Straße. The Palace of Justice is the large building on the right after 800 metres.

Memorium Nuremberg Trials, Bärenschanzstraße 72,
90429 Nuremberg, Germany
Tel: +49 (0)911 321 - 79 372   Fax: +49 (0)911 321 - 79 373
Email: memorium@stadt.nuernberg.de

The memorial is open 10.00am to 6.00pm while the last admission is at 5.00pm (closed Tuesday). However, Courtroom 600, where the trials were held, is still used as a court and visits cannot be guaranteed.

INDEX